FRANK WEDEKIND

Born in Hanover in 1864, Frank Wedek
universities of Lausanne, Munich and Z
mainly in Munich, where most of his pla
and where he died in 1918. Renowned for the sexual
explicitness of his work, he was a tireless experimenter,
borrowing elements from cabaret, circus, naturalism and
expressionism.

Because of its candid treatment of pubescent sexuality, one
of his earliest plays, *Spring Awakening*, was not seen on stage
until Max Reinhardt produced it in Berlin in 1906, fifteen
years after it was first written. His *Lulu* plays were seen earlier
– in 1898 and 1904 – and provided the basis for G.W.Pabst's
famous silent film, *Pandora's Box* (1928), which made a
legend out of Louise Brooks. Subsequent plays staged during
Wedekind's lifetime include *The Tenor* (1899), *The Marquis
of Keith* (1901), *Such is Life* (1902), *Musik* (1908) and *Castle
Wetterstein* (1917).

NICHOLAS WRIGHT

Nicholas Wright's plays include *Vincent in Brixton* (Olivier
Award for Best New Play, 2003) and the original production of
Mrs Klein, both at the National Theatre, in the West End and in
New York; *Treetops* and *One Fine Day* at Riverside Studios;
The Gorky Brigade at the Royal Court; *The Crimes of Vautrin*
for Joint Stock; *The Custom of the Country* and *The Desert Air*
for the RSC; *Cressida* for the Almeida and *The Reporter* at the
National. Adaptations include *His Dark Materials*, *Three
Sisters* and *John Gabriel Borkman* for the National; *Thérèse
Raquin* at Chichester Festival Theatre and the National; and
Naked and *Lulu* at the Almeida. He wrote the libretti for Rachel
Portman's opera *The Little Prince* (Houston Grand Opera) and
for Jonathan Dove's opera for television, *Man on the Moon*,
based on the Apollo 11 moon landing. Other writing for
television includes adaptations of *More Tales of the City* and
The No. 1 Ladies' Detective Agency (BBC/HBO). His writing
about the theatre includes *99 Plays*, a personal view of
playwriting from Aeschylus to the present day, and *Changing
Stages: A View of British Theatre in the Twentieth Century*, co-
written with Richard Eyre.

Other Titles in this Series

Victoria Benedictsson
THE ENCHANTMENT
  in a version by Clare Bayley

Anton Chekhov
THE CHERRY ORCHARD
  trans. Stephen Mulrine
THE SEAGULL
  trans. Stephen Mulrine
THREE SISTERS
  in a version by Nicholas Wright
UNCLE VANYA
  trans. Stephen Mulrine

Johann Wolfgang von Goethe
FAUST – PARTS ONE & TWO
  in a version by Howard Brenton

Nikolai Gogol
THE GOVERNMENT
INSPECTOR
  trans. Stephen Mulrine

Maxim Gorky
CHILDREN OF THE SUN
  trans. Stephen Mulrine

Henrik Ibsen
A DOLL'S HOUSE
  trans. Kenneth McLeish
AN ENEMY OF THE PEOPLE
  in a version by Arthur Miller
GHOSTS
  trans. Stephen Mulrine
HEDDA GABLER
  in a version by Richard Eyre
JOHN GABRIEL BORKMAN
  in a version by Nicholas Wright
THE LADY FROM THE SEA
  trans. Kenneth McLeish
THE MASTER BUILDER
  trans. Kenneth McLeish
PEER GYNT
  trans. Kenneth McLeish
ROSMERSHOLM
  in a version by Mike Poulton
THE WILD DUCK
  trans. Stephen Mulrine

Gotthold Ephraim Lessing
NATHAN THE WISE
  in a version by Edward Kemp

Molière
DON JUAN
  trans. Kenneth McLeish
EDUCATING AGNES
('The School for Wives')
  in a version by Liz Lochhead
THE HYPOCHONDRIAC
  trans. Martin Sorrell
THE LEARNED LADIES
  trans. A. R. Waller
THE MISER
  trans. Martin Sorrell
MISERYGUTS & TARTUFFE
  in versions by Liz Lochhead
SCAPINO
  trans. Jeremy Sams

Edmond Rostand
CYRANO DE BERGERAC
  in a version by Anthony Burgess

Friedrich Schiller
DON CARLOS
  in a version by Mike Poulton
MARY STUART
  in a version by Jeremy Sams

August Strindberg
THE DANCE OF DEATH
  trans. Stephen Mulrine
A DREAM PLAY
  in a version by Caryl Churchill
THE FATHER
  in a version by Mike Poulton
MISS JULIE
  trans. Kenneth McLeish

Franz Wedekind
SPRING AWAKENING
  trans. Julian and Margarete Forsyth

Émile Zola
THÉRÈSE RAQUIN
  in a version by Nicholas Wright

Frank Wedekind

LULU

in a new version by
Nicholas Wright
from a translation by Wes Williams

NICK HERN BOOKS
London

www.nickhernbooks.co.uk

A Nick Hern Book

This version of Frank Wedekind's *Lulu* was first published in Great Britain as a paperback original in 2001 by Nick Hern Books Limited, The Glasshouse, 49a Goldhawk Road, London W12 8QP

Reprinted 2004, 2005, 2006, 2007, 2011, 2014

Lulu © by Nicholas Wright
Introduction © by Nicholas Wright

Nicholas Wright has asserted his rights to be identified as author of this work

This version from a literal translation by Wes Williams

Front cover image: photo by Hugo Glendinning; design by AKA

Typeset by Country Setting, Kingsdown, Kent, CT14 8ES
Printed in Great Britain by Mimeo Ltd, St Ives, Cambs PE27 3LE

A CIP catalogue record for this book is available from the British Library

ISBN 978 1 85459 453 2

Lulu, in this adaptation by Nicholas Wright from a translation by Wes Williams, was first presented by the Almeida Theatre on 1 March 2001. Press night was 8 March. The cast was as follows:

Dr. Franz Schoning	Alan Howard
Eduard Schwarz	James Hillier
Chief Medical Officer Dr. Goll	Roger Swaine
Lulu	Anna Friel
Alwa Schoning	Oliver Milburn
Schigolch	Tom Georgeson
Henrietta	Imogen Slaughter
Dr. Bernstein	Leon Lissek
Martha, Countess of Geschwitz	Johanna ter Steege
Rodrigo Quast	Andrew Ufondu
Ferdinand	Jason Pitt
Puntschu	Leon Lissek
Madeleine de Marelle	Marella Oppenheim
Kadega	Anna Maguire
	Francesca Murray-Fuentes
The Marquis Casti-Piani	James Faulkner
Bianetta Gazil	Samia Akudo
Ludmila Steinherz	Imogen Slaughter
Bob, Lulu's groom	Sid Mitchell
The Chief of Police	Jason Pitt
Mr. Hopkins	Roger Swaine
Jack	Peter Sullivan

Direction Jonathan Kent
Design Rob Howell
Lighting Mark Henderson
Music Jonathan Dove
Sound John A Leonard

Divine Birth

Frank Wedekind (1864–1918) was playwright, journalist, songwriter, cabaret performer, actor, dissident and roué. Most of these qualities ran in the family. He was conceived in San Francisco, the son of a German political exile and his second wife, a German actress and singer who was touring the Wild West rather in the style (one imagines) of Marlene Dietrich in *Destry Rides Again*. When they married, she was exactly half her husband's age, 'a fact which strikes me as not altogether devoid of significance', Wedekind wrote later. The couple returned to Europe in time for their son to be born on German soil, where he was christened 'Benjamin Franklin' in honour of the American democratic tradition.

He was 26 when he wrote his beautiful paean to sexual freedom, *Spring Awakening*: the play which would make his name when it was finally produced by Max Reinhardt fifteen years later. Meanwhile he moved to Paris, on the proceeds of his father's will. The walls of the Paris galleries were dripping with brand-new Renoirs, Monets and Gauguins, Sarah Bernhardt and Réjane were at their height and Debussy had just had his first success but none of these names seems to have interested him. He spent his energies writing and having sex, with a distinct bias in each case towards avant-garde experiment. 'I can hardly speak because my tongue is fearfully sore. It's at least a centimetre longer than it was,' he wrote in his diary after a night with a young prostitute named Margot. It seems the damage wasn't serious, since he soon found himself being carried away by the 'imperious Olympian grandeur' of a young cocotte named Alice. 'She whinnied like a foal,' he noted. But accidents will happen. 'I shove my lower jaw back into place and discover I've torn a ligament,' he wrote.

On 12 June 1892 he was walking down the Champs Elysées when he had the idea for a new play, 'a gruesome tragedy'. He skipped a date with a couple of friends at Yvette Guilbert's and drafted Act One instead. Three more acts followed, under the working title of *Astarte*. In January 1894, he left for a six-month stay in London, and it was here that he wrote the fifth and final act of his profound and ambiguous masterpiece. Its working title in London was *Divine Birth*. When he'd finished the play, he called it *Pandora's Box: a Monster Tragedy*. But by a series of accidents and appropriations, oddly like the process by which its central character is re-named at the whim of each new lover, the play has acquired a different title in the public mind: *Lulu*.

Wedekind's life, post-*Lulu*, was avid and adventurous. He was a star contributor to the satiric periodical 'Simplicissimus' and served a seven-month stretch of imprisonment for making fun of the Kaiser. He sang and perfomed in alternative cabaret, wrote prolifically and became notorious as a political and sexual plainspeaker. Persistence paid off, and when he turned fifty he was feted throughout Germany. Bertolt Brecht, then a promising young local poet, was one of his circle and stood at the graveside when Wedekind died at the age of 53. But the younger writer's published tribute had a touch of envy about it: 'His greatest work was his personality,' he declared.

Wedekind's *Monster Tragedy* was never produced in his lifetime in the form that he'd written it: in a way, it was his own tragedy too. The reason is obvious. It's a disturbing play even to the modern eye, and what it must have seemed like to a publisher, producer or government censor of the 1890's is easy to imagine. No-one would touch it. Wedekind's response was to rewrite the play, again and again, and in the process to lose his focus. It was 'development hell': the gut-wrenching process which modern screenwriters undergo of seeing their work pulled apart by butter-fingered script-doctors, with the added cruelty that in this case the script-doctor was the writer himself. Long passages were cut, changed and diluted, new characters added, the plot became ever more tortuous. Worst of all, he cut the play down the middle, thus turning it into two separate plays: *Earth-Spirit* and (confusingly, the second of the two) *Pandora's Box*. He then added a new and redundant act to each.

Publication, production and the odd prosecution followed. Even in their mutilated form, the plays caused enough of a sensation to inspire Berg's great opera and no fewer than five silent movies, including the Pabst masterpiece. Wedekind acted in the plays whenever he could, sometimes as Dr. Schön (as Dr. Schoning was renamed), sometimes as the new character of the Ringmaster, sometimes as Jack – and it was in the course of playing Jack in a single club-performance of *Pandora's Box* organised by Karl Kraus in Vienna, that he fell in love with Tilly Newes, the actress playing Lulu. They married the following year: at 19, she was just under half his age.

After Wedekind's death, the usual procedure for anyone wanting to present *Lulu* was to run the two-play version together . . . why leave anything out? . . . and then to cut it down to performable length: hence the play's reputation as a wonderful idea brought low by muddled writing. One such version was planned (though never produced) at the Royal Court in the early '60's, in a translation by Christopher Isherwood. A few years later, when I was working there, and rather addicted to going through old files, I came across a batch of letters from Wedekind's and Tilly Newes' daughter Kadidja, urging the Court to present, not a corrupted version of the play, but one close to her father's original vision, one which she herself had reconstructed and would be only too happy to provide. One got the impression that her life was a frustrating one, trying to persuade the world that she wasn't just one of those power-crazed copyright-holders who can't bear to give up control. She was vindicated in the 1980's, when a full and scholarly reconstruction was published in Germany, and produced by Peter Zadek in Hamburg.

I read this version in my office at the National Theatre, in the late '80's, in Wes Williams' translation – the same translation on which I have based the adaptation published here. I will never forget the thrill of turning the pages. I knew and loved the two-play epic – indeed, the only reason I was reading Wedekind's original was as scholarly back-up for a production which the National was planning in a version by Angela Carter. (Also never produced.) But this new text was different. It was clearer and odder, more accessible and more extreme. And it was far, far more beautiful. Huge cascades of dialogue unfolded – urgent, quickfire exchanges. In their staccato rhythm, they echoed the beating heart, the shock of sudden contact, the shudder of desire. A sense of physical reality emerged, where before there had been the clash of figures in an expressionist vacuum. And the action shot forward like an arrow.

Strangely, it now turned out that, in the original version, Wedekind had written the Paris and London acts in the language which the characters themselves would have spoken: the Parisians converse in French, Lulu's London customers (and Lulu herself, when dealing with them) speak English. Wedekind's French was good, his English less so. Yet the 'Jack' scene, written in hesitant, formal, foreigner's English, is ravishing.

There are many things about this play which are disturbing and magical, which hint at strangenesses beyond the written text, but (for me) nothing is so evocative as the exchanges between client and hooker which Wedekind didn't invent, which he simply transcribed. They're too convincing to be have been written in any other way. 'You say, you missed the last bus and that you have spend the night with one of your friends.' 'I had a rich friend – give me your shilling.' 'Are you a bugger?' Some long-forgotten London prostitute said these words to a client she probably never met again: a hawk-nosed, deep-eyed, burly young German, who afterwards wrote them down as well as he could remember, sometimes accurately, sometimes (as in the first example) pitted with Teutonic blunders. These fragments of lost lives seem to me to be precious, and I've changed them as little as possible, though I know the effect is odd.

Such other changes as I have made consist of discreet cuts – since even this five-act version would take around four hours to perform in full – and patches of (I hope) invisible mending where Wedekind's indifference to consistent plotting produced results which seemed to me to verge on the impenetrable. I've done nothing to stoke up the sexuality of the play, or bring it 'up to date': this is how it was.

The play retains its mystery. It belongs to that small club of plays – of which *Hamlet* is perhaps the founder member –

whose meaning is precisely embodied in the personality of a luminous but enigmatic central character, and thus can never be quite pinned down. Just as Lulu the woman is transformed by each lover into the embodiment of his own desires, so *Lulu* the play transforms itself to fit the preconceptions of its audience. (And no doubt those of its adaptor.) Is Lulu a lethal love-goddess, dealing death to all who enter her circle of enchantment? Angela Carter, in a brilliant essay, has a lot of fun with this view: it's just the invention (she argues) of men who can't cope with what they lust for. 'Desire does not so much transcend its object as ignore it completely in favour of a fantastic recreation of it.' And *femmes fatales*, as she rightly points out, aren't noted for walking the streets (as Lulu does) in order to support perfectly able-bodied men who can't be bothered to earn a living. Is Lulu, then, a woman whose only sin is to be healthily-sexed, and whose fate is to be exploited by a string of heartless men?

But Lulu is more than that: she's a creature of infinite colours, drawn (surely) from the many women whom Wedekind met on his sexual odyssey – some irresistible, some fearlessly honest, some devious, some manic, all doomed. Certainly he must have come across a woman who, at the age of five or so, was raped and prostituted by a man who may have been her father. This is exactly what happened to Lulu, as Wedekind goes to some trouble to spell out. Is he saying that this hideous event has formed her life, that it's made her what she is as an adult? As a 19th-century buck, he may not have spotted the connection. Yet his comments on women are full of insight, and the way that Lulu sexualises every relationship she enters into with a man seems very much part of the damaged-child syndrome.

This is what sprang out at me most starkly while I was working through the play, and it amazed me that no-one who'd written about the play seemed to have called attention to it. But that's what *Lulu* is like: you find what you look for.

Nicholas Wright

Characters

In Germany

DR. FRANK SCHONING, *a newspaper editor*
EDUARD SCHWARZ, *a painter*
Chief Medical Officer DR. GOLL
LULU
ALWA SCHONING
HENRIETTA, *a maid*
SCHIGOLCH, *perhaps Lulu's father*
DR. BERNSTEIN
MARTHA, *Countess of Geschwitz*
RODRIGO QUAST, *an acrobat*
FERDINAND, *Lulu's coachman*

In Paris

PUNTSCHU, *a banker*
MADELEINE DE MARELLE
KADEGA, *her daughter*
THE MARQUIS CASTI-PIANI
BIANETTA GAZIL
LUDMILA STEINHERZ
BOB, *Lulu's under-footman*
THE CHIEF OF POLICE
Gendarmes and party guests

In London

MR. HOPKINS
JACK

ACT ONE

Summer. A painter's studio. Canvases are stacked up. There's a dais for models to pose on. A Spanish screen, armchairs, an ottoman, Turkish pillows, a tiger-skin rug, a step-ladder.

SCHWARZ, *a painter, watches as* DR. SCHONING *inspects a portrait of a woman of forty.* SCHWARZ *has a photograph in his hand.*

SCHONING. There's something wrong. I can't quite place it. The woman I married was more than this.

SCHWARZ. It isn't easy working from a photograph, Dr. Schoning. If I'd seen her in life, I could have . . .

SCHONING. My wife would never have sat for a portrait. She would have thought of it as giving too much value to ephemeral things. Youth. The flesh.

He looks more closely.

I can't fault the likeness. It's the essence which is missing. Show me the photograph.

SCHWARZ *does.* SCHONING *looks at it.*

Look at these eyes. Try to imagine them in life. You see, beyond them, something eternal. Something uncorrupted by the material values of the world.

SCHWARZ. Perhaps if you took a few steps back . . . ?

SCHONING *walks backwards and knocks into another canvas.*

SCHONING. I'm sorry . . .

SCHWARZ *picks up the canvas.*

SCHWARZ. No, it's nothing.

SCHONING *sees the picture. He's startled.*

SCHONING. Good God!

SCHWARZ. Do you know her?

SCHONING. I think I've met her. Is she sitting for you?

SCHWARZ. She's Dr. Goll's new wife. He's commissioned a portrait. Take a look.

He lifts the painting on to the easel. It shows a young woman in a revealing Pierrot costume, holding a shepherd's crook.

Incredible, isn't it? The first time that fat little porker brought her in, I nearly fainted. I had to hang on to my easel. And when she got into that costume . . .

SCHONING. You must be used to women wearing less than this.

SCHWARZ. Oh, if you've seen one naked woman, you've seen them all.

Looking at the portrait:

She's different. She's like a nude with clothes on. I can't stop thinking about what's underneath. The way she lifts her foot or tilts her head . . . my heart starts pounding.

SCHONING. The soul evaporates. The body sweats. The fig-leaf stirs.

SCHWARZ. I'll show you the costume.

He moves away.

SCHONING (*to himself*). He ought to get out more often.

SCHWARZ *produces the costume.*

SCHWARZ. Low at the back. And . . . low at the front.

SCHONING *looks at it.*

SCHONING. Enormous pom-poms!

SCHWARZ *strokes them.*

SCHWARZ. Black velvet.

SCHONING. Like ravens in the snow.

   SCHWARZ *holds the costume up by the shoulders.*

SCHWARZ. No corset.

SCHONING. Strapless, too.

SCHWARZ. She doesn't need straps.

SCHONING. How does she put it on?

SCHWARZ. One, two, three. Climbs in.

SCHONING. What stops it falling down?

SCHWARZ. It doesn't.

SCHONING. Isn't it bound to? There's nothing holding it up.

SCHWARZ. It's the way she holds her shoulder.

SCHONING. The trouser-legs . . .

SCHWARZ. You've noticed.

SCHONING . . . . are uncommonly wide. One more inch . . .

SCHWARZ. She hitches the left one up to just below . . .

SCHONING. Below . . . ?

SCHWARZ . . . . the knee.

SCHONING . . . . while the right leg covers her foot . . .

SCHWARZ . . . . to the end of her toes . . .

SCHONING . . . . with satin shoes . . .

SCHWARZ . . . . and black silk stockings . . .

SCHONING . . . . clear as glass . . .

SCHWARZ . . . . and then I'm supposed to concentrate on painting?

   He turns to the painting:

   Look at that arm . . .

SCHONING . . . . stretched out with such an elegant air . . .

SCHWARZ . . . . it's like a jewel . . . cut to perfection . . . the whiteness of the inner elbow . . . the light blue veins . . . the bloom of the skin . . . and then the armpits . . .

SCHONING. Yes . . . ?

SCHWARZ . . . . each with a single lock of hair inside it . . .

SCHONING (*looking at the canvas*). . . . . though you haven't yet filled them in.

SCHWARZ. They're dyed!

SCHONING. Dyed?

SCHWARZ. Jet black!

SCHONING. Nonsense.

SCHWARZ. They're darker there than anywhere else . . .

SCHONING. What 'anywhere else' else did you have in mind?

SCHWARZ folds up the costume.

SCHWARZ. Well, perhaps not dyed. But she certainly clips them into shape.

SCHONING. And while you're painting . . . are you alone?

SCHWARZ. Oh no . . . her husband sits and guards her.

SCHONING. So he should . . .

SCHWARZ . . . . with people like us around.

He hangs the costume up.

SCHONING (*to himself*). With people like us . . .

SCHWARZ. They'll soon be here. Don't you want to meet her?

SCHONING. Not this morning.

He turns to the portrait of his wife. Dismissive.

Don't bother with that any more. It's fine. Just frame it.

SCHWARZ. In something suitably austere? Not too ornate?

SCHONING. Whatever you like. I'll find my own way out.
If . . .

In the doorway, he almost collides with DR. GOLL *and*
LULU.

GOLL. Good morning to you, Schoning. What in the devil's
name brings *you* here?

SCHONING (*to* GOLL). Herr Schwarz is doing a memorial
portrait of my wife.

GOLL. Of course, forgive me. (*Of* SCHONING *and* LULU.)
You two are of course acquainted.

SCHONING. Frau Goll.

He kisses her hand.

Where was it we met last time?

LULU. It was at Easter. At the Countess Villa-Franca's. Where's
my costume?

She moves away.

SCHWARZ. Here.

GOLL. Good morning, Schwarz.

SCHONING. Good day to you, Goll.

LULU. Are you going?

SCHONING. I mustn't disturb you. Aren't you about to
change?

LULU. That's all the more reason for you to stay.

GOLL. Please do, please do.

LULU *gives her hat and coat to* SCHWARZ. *Meanwhile, to*
SCHONING*:*

I'm sorry about your wife. Speaking as her doctor, I would
have sworn that she would pull through. Her heart was
sound. She needed, perhaps, some kind of stimulus that
I couldn't provide.

SCHONING *and* LULU *exchange a glance.*

SCHONING. Don't we all?

GOLL. Not you, not you! Running a newspaper is excitement enough for anyone.

SCHONING. It's only the same excitement day after day. And new excitements don't come knocking on one's door. One has to look for them.

LULU (*to* SCHONING). You ought to look a bit harder, Dr. Schoning.

SCHONING. I also lack the opportunity.

GOLL. Popsy, get ready. Our painter here is licking his brush in high anticipation.

LULU. Posing's boring.

GOLL. Think of the pleasure you give to others.

LULU. I always do.

SCHWARZ stands by the bedroom door, costume in hand.

SCHWARZ. If you would be so kind . . . ?

LULU (*to* SCHONING). Don't go.

She takes the costume and goes into the bedroom.

GOLL. You see I call her 'Popsy'.

SCHONING. I thought 'Mignon' suited her well.

GOLL. 'Mignon'? No, 'Popsy''s better, from my personal point of view. I have a weakness for the incomplete . . . the immature . . . the innocent child in need of fatherly protection.

SCHONING. And the wife who never leaves her husband feeling guilty.

GOLL. And who never attempts to take control.

SCHONING. While the advantages of married life remain.

GOLL. Yes . . . at my age, one feels the chill proximity of the Reaper. But there are certain needs one never escapes. Quite so, quite so.

SCHONING *glances towards the bedroom door.*

SCHONING. She's taking her time getting into that costume.

GOLL. Getting it off is faster. I stand behind and play the lady's maid.

SCHONING. Did you design it?

GOLL. I prescribed it. Not on medical grounds, I do assure you. It's distinctly hazardous for a man in my state of health.

LULU *comes out of the bedroom in her Pierrot costume.*

LULU. How do I look?

GOLL. You are the cynosure of eyes, my dearest! Schwarz, one moment.

He takes SCHWARZ *away and out of earshot.*

LULU (*to* SCHONING). Well?

SCHONING. You're amazing.

He moves closer.

I haven't heard from you in months.

LULU. Not so close. He's got eyes like a hawk.

SCHONING. When can I see you?

LULU. He watches me all the time. I can't get away.

GOLL *calls over:*

GOLL. I'm telling our artist friend he must avoid the Impressionist style. I want no daubs, no dots, no flicks of the brush. Those tricks can never convey the flesh-tones.

SCHONING. It depends who's doing the flicking.

GOLL (*to* LULU). Roll your panties up. I wouldn't trust this fellow not to paint them.

LULU. I'm not wearing any.

SCHWARZ. This way, if you please.

She goes on to the dais.

GOLL (*to* SCHONING). She looks better from this angle.

He leads SCHONING *round.*

LULU. I look better from every angle. (*To* SCHONING.)
Don't you pity me, Dr. Schoning?

SCHONING. I'd give my soul to *be* you.

LULU. Could *you* stay stiff as a post for two whole hours?

SCHONING. I could certainly try.

SCHWARZ. The knee a little forward. Yes, like that.

He re-arranges her. Meanwhile:

GOLL (*of Schwarz*). I'm throwing my money away. The man's
an idiot.

SCHONING. I envy artists. They know what they are. They
sleep at night surrounded by things they've made. Besides,
you can't be harsh on a man who lives from hand to mouth.
I'd like to help him.

GOLL. How?

SCHONING. Oh . . . give him a chance, and see if he's got the
wit to take it. Though he'll probably live to curse me if he
does.

SCHWARZ (*to* LULU). The hand quite still.

He starts to paint.

GOLL. A warm, romantic touch is what is required this
morning.

SCHONING. Think of the subject as a still life. Like a ripe
fruit served up to you on a silver platter.

SCHWARZ *drops his brush.*

GOLL. *Now* what's wrong?

SCHWARZ. Nothing.

He paints.

GOLL. The role of art is to embody our noblest aspirations. (*To* SCHONING.) Most modern exhibitions make me want to neuter myself like a tom-cat.

SCHONING. Why do you go to them?

GOLL. That's what I ask myself. Perhaps it's this sultry weather we've been having.

Pause. SCHWARZ *paints with as much concentration as he can muster.*

SCHONING. I hear the O'Murphy girl is dancing tonight at the Varieties.

GOLL. She's doing her Peruvian pearl-fisher act. I've seen it before. Prince Polossowski took me along.

SCHONING. He's the fattest pearl that *she'll* ever find.

GOLL. His beard has gone boot-black with happiness. The Opera's good at present.

SCHONING. I couldn't face the boredom.

GOLL. Try it! That's your doctor's recommendation.

SCHONING. I'm already taking your sleeping-pills.

A knock at the door.

GOLL. Opera won't corrode your stomach-lining, and your sleep will be all the sounder.

SCHONING. Somebody's knocking.

SCHWARZ. Excuse me.

He puts down his brush and goes to the door.

GOLL (*to* LULU). Smile! Go on. What else were sugary lips created for? (*Indicating Schwarz.*) You're safe with *that* little eunuch.

ALWA SCHONING *comes in.*

ALWA. May I come in?

SCHWARZ. Please do.

LULU. Your son has arrived, Dr. Schoning.

ALWA *sees her.*

ALWA. Frau Goll?

LULU. You remember me?

ALWA. Could I forget you? (*To* GOLL.) Good morning,
  Doctor. (*To* SCHONING.) Good morning, father.

SCHONING. Why are you here?

ALWA. You said you wanted to see my dress-rehearsal.

SCHONING. You told me that was Sunday.

LULU. No, the first *performance* is on Sunday.

GOLL. How do you know?

LULU. I've seen the posters.

GOLL. What is the title of your show?

ALWA. 'Zarathustra'.

GOLL. 'Zarathustra'? I thought that he was in a mad-house.

SCHONING. My son's new challenge to theatrical convention
  is a dance extravaganza inspired by the works of Friedrich
  Nietzsche.

GOLL. He's a philosopher, surely? A repulsive fellow. I've
  seen him skipping around the town on crutches.

ALWA. Act Two is based on Nietzsche's 'Dancing Song.' It
  starts with the wood-nymphs in the forest. Zarathustra
  tiptoes through the bushes. Then the dew descends . . .

GOLL. Who dreamed this up?

SCHONING. My brilliant son.

ALWA. Act One is called 'At the Sign of the Colourful Cow'.
  There's a tight-rope walker, wild dogs, crippled authority,
  foolish virgins . . .

GOLL. Virgins, eh?

ALWA . . . . the Last Man on Earth, the Guardians of the Night
   and the Snorting Pig . . .

GOLL (*to* SCHONING). I wonder . . .

ALWA (*carries on*). . . . . then: Zarathustra, burying the
   tightrope dancer in the market-place!

GOLL. That won't shock us. Nothing's shocking any longer.

ALWA. Act Three: the Dog of Fire is spewed out of the
   volcano, along with the trolls. They're covered in sacks
   right down to the waist. Their legs are bare.

GOLL. Their legs are bare . . . ?

ALWA. The serpent appears! Behold! The Ubermensch is
   born.

SCHONING. She's danced by Corticelli.

GOLL. Oh, la Corticelli? She's not wearing a sack, I hope?

ALWA. I've had to put her in a veil. The police insisted.

GOLL. Will she be there for the dress rehearsal?

ALWA. They'll all be there. Do you want to come?

SCHONING (*to* GOLL). We'll have to leave at once.

ALWA. You can go backstage. You can pass your observations
   on to the Snorting Pig.

GOLL. I'd only want to meet la Corticelli.

SCHONING. She'd be delighted.

GOLL. Would she? Then I . . . No, it's impossible. I'll come
   back here and find this bungler's ruined the painting.

ALWA. He can't ruin much in half a morning.

SCHONING. He can always cover it up.

GOLL. No! Next time!

ALWA. Allons!

   He's about to go.

LULU. Keep us a box for Sunday.

ALWA. Oh, I will.

GOLL. Take my carriage! Give my regards to La . . . No! I've changed my mind. (*To* LULU.) Popsy, my dear, Piggy is going for walkies. Bye bye.

LULU. Squeak squeak.

GOLL. Oink oink.

SCHONING. Good morning to you, Frau Goll.

LULU (*to* SCHONING). Good morning.

ALWA, *Dr.* SCHONING *and Dr.* GOLL *leave.* SCHWARZ *paints. After a few moments:*

La Corticelli must be something special.

SCHWARZ. She's just a . . .

LULU. Just a what?

SCHWARZ *paints.*

SCHWARZ. Nothing.

LULU. Do you know her?

SCHWARZ. Certainly not!

LULU. She must have something. My husband's never . . .

SCHWARZ. What?

LULU. He's never left me alone before.

SCHWARZ. What happens when he goes to see his patients?

LULU. He's got a housekeeper. She never leaves me alone. She baths me, she does my hair and she tucks me up in bed. And when she's had a drink . . . her hands start wandering.

SCHWARZ. Why don't you sack her?

LULU. I can't.

SCHWARZ. Why not?

LULU. I'd have nobody to dress me for my dancing lessons.

SCHWARZ. Couldn't you dress yourself?

LULU. I wouldn't know what costume suits me best. I don't know what I am.

SCHWARZ. What does she dress you in?

LULU. As little as possible.

He stops painting.

Don't stop!

SCHWARZ. Do you change your costume for every dance?

LULU. I have two rooms completely full of costumes.

SCHWARZ. When do you dance?

LULU. After dinner.

SCHWARZ. Every evening?

LULU. Every evening.

SCHWARZ. Tell me about it. Painting's easier when the subject's talking.

LULU. Sometimes I'm dressed like a fisherman's boy. I wear a linen shirt unbuttoned down the front. And very short trousers, widely cut.

SCHWARZ. Who's your dancing-master?

LULU. He is.

SCHWARZ. Goll?

He lets his paint-brush slip.

LULU. My husband. Paint!

SCHWARZ *paints.*

SCHWARZ. I'd like to see him dance for you some time.

LULU. He knows all the steps. The czarda. The tango. The gopak. The waltz. He names the dance. I do it. While he watches.

SCHWARZ *falters.*

Keep going! He might come back any minute.

SCHWARZ. Aren't you disgusted?

LULU. By what?

SCHWARZ. By married life.

LULU. Oh no. Every Thursday Count Polossowski comes to
watch. Doctor Schoning came once too. I dressed as Eve.

SCHWARZ. As *Eve*?

LULU. I wore . . . red lace-up boots. Mauve stockings. And
my hair was tied with a crimson bow.

SCHWARZ. I can't go on.

LULU. Why not?

SCHWARZ. My arm's gone stiff.

LULU. It's never gone stiff before.

SCHWARZ. We're losing the light.

LULU. We can do it in the dark.

SCHWARZ. Aren't you freezing?

LULU. I wear much less than this at home. When he's at work,
I wear a petticoat. It's been too hot for anything else.
Yesterday I wore a dark green silk kimono. With pale green
stockings. A scarf in my hair of delicate pink, and garters
that were even paler.

SCHWARZ. You were dressed like a tart.

LULU. I like to be comfortable. Then I can breathe. Like now.
Just look . . .

She breathes in.

You see?

SCHWARZ. Don't do that!

He throws down his brush. Walks about.

I wish I was a shoe-shine boy. Then I'd only have feet to
look at. Why did your husband go to that damned rehearsal?

LULU. He won't be long.

SCHWARZ (*at the easel*). The paint won't stick. It's melting off the canvas.

LULU. Carry on!

SCHWARZ. The colours are dancing before my eyes.

LULU. Keep going.

SCHWARZ. Oh yes, keep going. He's the boss of the Medical School. He could declare me morally deficient. All right, I'll try.

He dabs a little paint on.

If you could lift . . . the trouser-leg a little.

LULU. Like this?

SCHWARZ. A fraction . . . higher.

LULU. You might see more than you bargained for.

SCHWARZ takes hold of a hand.

SCHWARZ. Like this.

LULU pushes her shepherd's crook in his face.

LULU. Don't touch me!

She runs towards the door.

SCHWARZ. Where are you going?

LULU. Leave me alone!

SCHWARZ. I was joking!

He advances her into the corner.

LULU. I know about jokes. That wasn't a joke. You won't get anywhere by forcing me.

SCHWARZ steps back.

SCHWARZ. I'm sorry.

LULU goes back to the dais.

LULU. Paint.

SCHWARZ *moves towards her.*

SCHWARZ. If you would . . . take up your position? Please? Frau Goll?

LULU. Get behind that easel.

He tries to embrace her: She escapes and takes shelter behind the ottoman.

SCHWARZ. You need spanking.

He advances on the ottoman.

LULU. You'll have to catch me first.

She moves around it.

SCHWARZ. Ten, nine, eight, seven . . . coming to get you!

LULU *darts out of his reach. Taunting him:*

LULU. Pussy pussy pussy!

He tries to trap her. She slips away.

Doo di doo di doo!

SCHWARZ. You'll pay for this!

LULU. Back to your easel, slave.

SCHWARZ *dives to the right, then to the left.*

SCHWARZ. Nearly got you . . .

LULU *dives to the left, then to the right.*

LULU. If I were wearing a dress I'd be quite helpless . . .

SCHWARZ . . . . teasy weasy . . .

LULU . . . . but I can run . . .

SCHWARZ . . . . just wait . . .

LULU . . . . because I've nothing on underneath!

SCHWARZ *takes a leap over the ottoman.*

SCHWARZ. Gotcha!

LULU *throws the tiger-skin over him, leaps over him and scampers up the stepladder.*

LULU. I'm flying! I can see all the cities of the world!

SCHWARZ *is climbing out from under the tiger-skin.*

SCHWARZ. Damn this fur.

LULU *holds on to the ladder with one hand: with the other, she reaches high into the air.*

LULU. I'm touching the clouds! I can reach the stars!

SCHWARZ *starts climbing the ladder. Things are getting rapidly unsafe.*

SCHWARZ. You're beautiful! Beautiful!

LULU. I'll tread on your fingers!

SCHWARZ. Careful!

LULU. God save Poland!

LULU *tips over the ladder . . . or somehow it tips over . . . and they land in a heap.* LULU *throws the Spanish blind (or something) over* SCHWARZ. *He lies groaning on the floor.*

LULU. Now keep your hands to yourself! Or *this* will happen!

And, on 'this', she throws at him both the portrait of SCHONING's *wife and the easel on which it was mounted. Severe damage results.*

SCHWARZ. Jesus Christ! My rent! My trip to Norway!

He makes a dash for her.

LULU. Catch me!

She leaps over the ottoman, over the collapsed step-ladder and walks delicately across the platform.

Mind the ditch!

She somersaults across the carpet, trips over the portrait and falls over. SCHWARZ *leaps on top of her.*

SCHWARZ. Victory!

She wriggles free.

LULU. Don't squash.

He gets up to chase her further.

Leave me alone. I'm fainting!

She collapses on to the ottoman. SCHWARZ *stares at her recumbent form. Then goes firmly to the door. Bolts it.*

SCHWARZ. 'Like a ripe fruit served up on a silver platter.' It's easy to say.

Pause.

Are you all right?

He lies down beside her on the ottoman. LULU *opens her eyes.*

LULU. I thought I was falling.

SCHWARZ *looks at her. Impulsively kisses her bare arm.*

SCHWARZ. Take off your costume.

LULU. It's cold in here.

He tries to slip off her costume.

No, don't.

SCHWARZ. Let's go.

LULU. Where to?

SCHWARZ. The bedroom.

LULU. He might come back.

SCHWARZ. Just for a moment.

LULU. What do you want?

SCHWARZ. I love you.

LULU. Oh . . .

She shudders. He brushes her trouser-leg.

SCHWARZ. You're wonderful.

She pushes his hand away.

LULU. Don't do that.

He kisses her.

SCHWARZ. Come on.

LULU. Let's stay here.

SCHWARZ. Get undressed. I want you. Let me. Let me do it.

LULU. Yes.

SCHWARZ. Oh Jesus!

LULU. Whatever you want.

After a few more moments, he draws away from her.

SCHWARZ. Don't *do* this to me!

LULU. Take me.

SCHWARZ. *Please*! *Please!*

LULU. What's the matter?

SCHWARZ. I'm not used to this. Help me. Be kind.

LULU. I'm *trying* to be kind.

SCHWARZ. Popsy . . . Popsy . . .

LULU. Don't call me that.

SCHWARZ. Mignon . . .

LULU. My name is Lulu.

SCHWARZ. I'll call you Eve.

LULU. Whatever you want.

SCHWARZ. Eve.

LULU. What do you want me to do?

SCHWARZ. Get undressed.

LULU. We don't need to.

SCHWARZ. You're teasing me.

LULU. I'm not, I'm not! Do you want to make love to me?

SCHWARZ. Eve . . .

LULU. Make love to me. Make love to me.

SCHWARZ. Eve . . .

LULU. What is it?

SCHWARZ. Please . . .

LULU. Don't you like me?

SCHWARZ (*wretched*). Oh God!

LULU. Come here, come here . . .

Stillness for a moment. The moment has gone.

Whatever you want.

Sharply, she moves away.

SCHWARZ (*shouts*). Oh Jesus Christ!

LULU (*terrified*). Don't kill me!

SCHWARZ (*quieter*). I'm sorry.

He moves away.

LULU. Is it *your* first time?

SCHWARZ looks at her in surprise.

SCHWARZ. Do you mean it's *yours* as well?

LULU. I . . .

Pause.

Yes.

SCHWARZ. Are you telling the truth?

There's a hammering on the door. GOLL's voice is heard:

GOLL. Open the door!

SCHWARZ springs up.

SCHWARZ. It's him!

LULU. He'll kill me!

Further hammering. Then the door falls crashing on to the floor. GOLL is revealed, his eyes bloodshot. He advances towards SCHWARZ, his stick raised threateningly.

GOLL. You dogs! You dogs!

He stops in his tracks. Then teeters and collapses on to the
floor. SCHWARZ *stands, shaking.* LULU, *who has fled to*
the door, stops and looks.

SCHWARZ. Doctor Goll?

Silence.

Herr Doctor Goll?

No answer.

I'll send for the doctor.

He goes out. LULU *stays where she is, some distance away*
from the body. Looks at it.

LULU. Then . . . *up* he jumps.

Silence. She whispers:

Piggy? Piggy?

She touches him with the tip of her toes.

Oink, oink.

To herself.

Two rooms of clothes . . . *I* don't know which ones to put on.

She bends over GOLL.

How strange his face looks now. As though I hardly knew
him. As though he might still burst in at any moment.
Who'll close his eyes?

SCHWARZ *comes back.*

SCHWARZ. Is he all right?

LULU. I think this time he really has gone walkies.

SCHWARZ *tries to lift the body.*

SCHWARZ. God, he's heavy.

He succeeds in turning the body round. To LULU,
indicating the ottoman.

Give me that cushion.

She does. He puts the cushion under GOLL*'s head.*

Doctor Goll?

To LULU*:*

He isn't moving.

LULU. What if I danced the tango?

SCHWARZ. Don't be tasteless.

LULU. Close his eyes.

SCHWARZ *stares at* GOLL.

SCHWARZ. Do you mean he's . . . *dead?*

He stares at GOLL *in comprehension.*

LULU. If he's not dead now, he never will be.

SCHWARZ. How can you talk like that?

LULU. It could be me next time. Or you. Go on, close them.
Be a man.

SCHWARZ *closes* GOLL*'s eyes.*

I'm going to be rich.

SCHWARZ *stares at her once more.*

SCHWARZ. Don't you have any feelings?

LULU. I'm only telling the truth.

SCHWARZ. Look at me.

He grasps her hands.

LULU. You're hurting.

SCHWARZ. Look into my eyes. What do you see?

LULU. I see . . . I see myself reflected back at me.

SCHWARZ. Tell me what else.

LULU. I don't know.

SCHWARZ. What are you?

LULU. I don't know.

SCHWARZ. Do you believe in God?

LULU. I don't know.

SCHWARZ. What *do* you believe in?

LULU. I don't know.

SCHWARZ. Have you a soul?

LULU. I don't know.

SCHWARZ. Are you a virgin?

LULU. I don't know.

SCHWARZ gets up and moves away.

What do you want me to tell you?

SCHWARZ. Everything.

LULU. Ever since I got married, I've danced half-naked every night.

SCHWARZ. Not that.

LULU. You asked.

SCHWARZ. Get dressed.

She goes out to the bedroom. SCHWARZ *looks at* GOLL.

I could help her. Foul as she is. Depraved as she is. But do I love her enough? Does she love me?

To GOLL:

Let's change places. You can take her back. Your dancing marionette. Your child. And while you're about it, take my youth. I'm finished with it.

LULU *opens the bedroom door. He looks up.*

What do you want?

LULU *indicates the back of her costume.*

LULU. Undo me.

End of Act One.

ACT TWO

An elegant drawing-room. Over the fireplace, in a magnificent frame, SCHWARZ's Pierrot portrait of LULU, now completed. A carved ebony desk, a Chinese table.

LULU and SCHWARZ are together in an armchair. She's in an eau-de-nil silk dress, very décolleté. She struggles to free herself.

LULU. Stop it!

SCHWARZ. You're my wife!

LULU. You're biting!

SCHWARZ. I can't help it.

LULU. Wait!

SCHWARZ. Till when?

LULU. Until this evening.

SCHWARZ. It's evening now.

LULU. But I want you properly.

SCHWARZ. What more can I give you?

LULU. You! Give me you!

SCHWARZ. I'm here!

LULU. No, not like this. Wait till the house is empty. We'll be free then. We can do what we want.

SCHWARZ. I want it now.

She struggles up.

LULU. Oh, do it yourself.

SCHWARZ. I've *never* done *that* !

He tries to lift up her dress. She holds it down.

LULU. I want to tell you something.

SCHWARZ. What?

LULU. It's a surprise.

SCHWARZ. I hate surprises. They're always bad. I can't wake up without imagining something dreadful's going to happen. That you'll be bitten by a mad dog. Or that the world will end, or the Government will collapse. It's always something that would take you away from me. What is it?

LULU. Listen.

She whispers in his ear.

SCHWARZ. I don't believe it.

She sits up, smiling.

LULU. Mm hm.

SCHWARZ. You! A mother?

LULU. Well, I will be.

SCHWARZ. Oh, Eve! Eve! Are you sure?

LULU. I've known for the last two weeks.

SCHWARZ. Why didn't you tell me?

LULU. I've been crying every night. I can't get rid of it. I've tried everything.

SCHWARZ. You must never do that! What for? I can support a family. I'm successful now. The dealers are fighting to buy whatever I paint. And while I fill the galleries of the world with Schwarzes, you, each year, will add another one to the nursery!

LULU. I feel that somebody's stopped the party just as I was beginning to enjoy it.

SCHWARZ. I must get back to work.

He collects his paintbrush and palette from the floor. Kisses LULU.

Until tonight.

LULU. I'm frightened.

SCHWARZ *laughs*.

SCHWARZ. I know you are!

LULU. Then what are you laughing at?

SCHWARZ. It isn't *my* fault you're having a baby.

LULU. Then whose fault is it?

SCHWARZ. Yours. Because there's something about you that I can't resist.

LULU. What?

SCHWARZ. I don't know. It's not the feel of your body. A man gets used to that.

LULU. My skin was softer before I met you. I used to run my finger-tips over my breasts, and leave pink stripes.

SCHWARZ. It isn't the way you twist about in bed. Though I adore it . . .

LULU. Perhaps it's my underwear. I'll stop wearing it.

SCHWARZ. God forbid! It isn't your kisses . . . though you're stingy with your kisses . . .

LULU *kisses him*.

SCHWARZ. Where did you learn to kiss like that?

LULU. In the same place you did.

She kisses him.

In the womb.

SCHWARZ. Is it your arms? Your legs? The way your body's put together?

He lifts her dress, so that her green stockings are visible to above the knee.

No it's not that.

LULU *protects herself.*

There's only one thing left that it can be.

LULU. Ssh.

SCHWARZ. Your . . .

She closes his mouth.

LULU. Don't say it.

SCHWARZ. It's your . . .

She chants nonsense to drown him out:

LULU. Doo di doo di doo.

SCHWARZ. You know what it is.

She sits up and crosses her legs.

LULU. Well I can't change *that.*

SCHWARZ *presses her to him.*

SCHWARZ. Don't! It's what you are! It's your soul!

He lays her gently in the armchair. They're about to make love.

LULU. Lock the door.

He goes to the door. As he's about to turn the key, the doorbell rings.

LULU. Let's say we're out.

SCHWARZ. It might be someone from the gallery.

They re-arrange themselves apart as HENRIETTA, *the maid, comes in.*

LULU. Who is it?

HENRIETTA. It's just a beggar, madam.

LULU. Let him come in. I'll give him something.

HENRIETTA *goes. To* SCHWARZ:

You go.

He goes out. LULU, *left alone, stares motionless ahead.*

LULU. It's *you.* You're here. That's good.

  SCHIGOLCH *comes in.*

SCHIGOLCH. You said your husband worked all morning.

LULU. Something came up. How much do you want this time?

SCHIGOLCH. Two hundred. Three if you've got it.

  LULU *goes to a desk, rummages in the drawers, finds
  money.*

SCHIGOLCH. Besides, I wanted to see where you'd landed up.

LULU. What do you think of it?

SCHIGOLCH. You've done all right for yourself.

  He shuffles his feet on the floor.

  Look at this carpet. My oh my.

LULU. When nobody's here, I walk around barefoot.

  SCHIGOLCH *sees the Pierrot painting.*

SCHIGOLCH. Is that you?

LULU. Don't you like it?

SCHIGOLCH. Maybe, maybe not. I'm no expert.

  He sits, looks round.

LULU. You'll want a drink, I expect.

SCHIGOLCH. I might, I might. What've you got?

LULU. Eau de Vie?

SCHIGOLCH. You know me. Whatever it is, I won't object.

  She pours him a drink.

  Is your husband a drinking man?

LULU. Of a sort.

SCHIGOLCH. What kind of sort? The sort that knocks you
  about?

LULU. The sort that falls into a stupor. Let's not talk about him. What's your news?

SCHIGOLCH. The streets get longer and my legs get shorter.

LULU. Have you still got your mouth-organ?

SCHIGOLCH. I do, I do. Fancy a tune?

He gets it out. Blows a few notes.

It's wheezy these days. Due for the scrap-heap, like its owner.

LULU. You've been on the scrap-heap as long as I've known you.

SCHIGOLCH. Just because the sun's gone down, it doesn't necessarily mean you get into bed. I'm looking forward to the winter. It might just finish me off, with luck.

LULU. Perhaps God's forgotten you.

SCHIGOLCH. He won't do that . . . he's got my name down. But there's too many others jumping the queue.

He strokes her knee.

When did I see you last . . . my Lulu . . . ?

LULU. Lulu!

SCHIGOLCH. What should I call you, if not Lulu?

LULU. Nobody's called me that since time began.

SCHIGOLCH. What are you now?

LULU. Eve.

SCHIGOLCH. Lulu . . . Mignon . . . Popsy . . . Eve . . .

LULU. That's what I answer to these days.

SCHIGOLCH. I always knew you'd land on your feet. What do you do all day?

LULU. I laze about. I sleep.

SCHIGOLCH. And then?

LULU. I stretch my joints . . . until they crack!

SCHIGOLCH. And when they've cracked?

LULU. Oh, what do you care?

SCHIGOLCH. Who knows you better than me? I found you. I protected you. I pinned my faith on you when all you had was a pair of liquid eyes and a nervous smile.

LULU. You make me sound like an animal.

SCHIGOLCH. And if you were an animal?

LULU. I'd be the finest. And the sleekest.

SCHIGOLCH. And the slinkiest. And the most refined.

LULU. Every night I rub my body with oil. Then I powder myself all over. Every inch of me is soft and clean.

SCHIGOLCH. As though you weren't a bucket of shite to start with.

LULU. When I slip between the sheets, I'm like an apple that's just been peeled.

SCHIGOLCH. You're a delicate fruit, that's true. A *poire hélène*. But what will you be in a year or two? You won't be fit for Animal Feeding Time. The beasts will turn their snouts up at you. You'll be zoo manure.

LULU takes his glass.

LULU. You've drunk enough.

SCHIGOLCH. I dragged you naked out of the slums.

LULU. You hung me up by the arms. You beat me with your belt till I was black and blue. Do you think I've forgotten all that?

SCHIGOLCH. It had to be done, my darling. Had to be done.

The doorbell rings.

LULU. Somebody's here.

He holds her chin up.

SCHIGOLCH. Adieu, ma petite duchesse.

LULU *kisses him.*

LULU. Adieu.

DR. SCHONING *comes in. To him:*

SCHIGOLCH. Adieu.

He goes.

SCHONING. What was your father doing here?

LULU. What's that's got to do with you?

SCHONING. If I were were your devoted husband, that old reprobate would never get past my doorstep.

LULU. What do you mean 'devoted'? What are you being so formal about? He's at the studio. Relax.

She sits, expecting him to relax at her side. He doesn't.

SCHONING. I had intended to convey this on my previous visit. But . . .

I . . .

LULU. If you mean 'yesterday', then say it.

SCHONING. Please listen to what I . . .

LULU. Well don't be so mysterious.

SCHONING. I'm come to request that your weekly visits . . .

LULU. What?

SCHONING. Your visits to me . . .

LULU. '*Visits*'?

SCHONING. 'Assignations' . . . 'rendezvous' . . . call them whatever you like . . . must end.

LULU. What's happened?

SCHONING. Nothing.

LULU. Then why are you talking in this peculiar way?

SCHONING. If you won't listen to me . . .

LULU. I am! I'm listening!

SCHONING. If you call at my house, my staff will refuse to admit you.

LULU. I see.

She gets up and walks up and down.

SCHONING. I shall, of course, preserve your reputation. The nature of our past relationship will be a private matter between the two of us. You have my word for that.

LULU *settles into a chair with admirable poise: one hand resting gracefully on the arm of the chair.*

LULU. I understand. You're getting married. Yes?

SCHONING. That is a factor.

LULU. May I ask the name of the lucky woman?

SCHONING. Fräulein zum Bergen.

LULU. Oh, her? How old is she, exactly?

SCHONING. She's young enough to be receptive to my guidance.

LULU. How does her mother feel about handing over a child like that to an old goat like you?

SCHONING. The Baroness has consented. I wouldn't describe her as enthusiastic.

LULU. But she owes you a favour.

SCHONING. She does.

LULU. If it wasn't for you, the Baron would have gone to prison.

SCHONING. He ought to have gone to prison. He's a swindler.

LULU. I suppose you paid your respects to the Baroness first, before moving on to her daughter?

SCHONING. It seemed only polite.

LULU. Well . . . we mustn't upset the poor woman any further. I won't come to your house.

SCHONING. Do you promise me that?

LULU. Why not? There are lots of other places we can meet.

SCHONING. We won't be meeting at all. Unless your husband's present.

LULU *is shocked*.

LULU. What?

SCHONING. Since he married you, I've grown to like him.

LULU. So have I!

SCHONING. I don't want to quarrel with him. He's a pleasant, harmless fellow. And he's . . . vulnerable. He's childlike.

LULU. He isn't like you and me, you mean. He's innocent.

SCHONING. That's putting it kindly. If he had a normally functioning brain, he'd have found out about the two of us long ago.

LULU. He's not an idiot. He's banal, that's all. He's gauche. He can't work out what's happening round him. And he's blind. He's blind as a chimney-stack.

SCHONING. Then you should take him in hand. That's what wives do.

LULU. I know that, thank you. I've been married before. Remember my poor little porker?

SCHONING. He spoiled you.

LULU. At least he wasn't banal.

SCHONING. He certainly wasn't. Remember his dancing-lessons?

LULU. And his big fat face getting redder and redder.

SCHONING. You want to return to the whip.

LULU. I dream about him all the time. I dream he's still alive. That he's come back to see me. Padding around the house in his stocking feet. He isn't angry any more. He's sad, that's all. The only thing he's upset about is that I've spent nearly all his money.

SCHONING. Well if this new one isn't up to the mark, you'll just have to improve him.

LULU. *How*?

SCHONING. Train him. Lead him on to a loftier plain.

LULU. He loves me.

SCHONING. Ah. Well that is fatal.

LULU. He wants me to have children.

SCHONING. Oh, your farmyard duties.

LULU. He calls me 'little mouse' and all the rest of it, and all the time he hasn't the faintest idea of who I am. He's never had a woman before. He unwraps me and puts me around his thing as though I was a contraceptive.

SCHONING. Have you any idea how many young girls would be grateful for that?

LULU. I wish he'd find one. God knows they're thick on the ground. On our wedding-night, he thought I was a virgin.

SCHONING. How did you manage that?

LULU. I yelled and he thought he'd hurt me.

SCHONING. And his self-esteem went rocketing.

LULU. It's been rocketing ever since. He's fine. If that's what's stopping you. You needn't worry about him.

SCHONING. Don't try to talk me round. My mind's made up. I can't afford a scandal.

LULU. We'll be discreet.

SCHONING. I want to carry my wife over a decent threshold.

LULU. She'll bore you senseless!

SCHONING. That's nothing to do with you. You have a fine young husband. With a brilliant future, thanks to me. Your standing in society is unquestioned. All I ask in return is that you leave me alone.

LULU. You don't want me any more! That's it, isn't it?

SCHONING. That's it.

LULU. No! No! I won't let you do this!

SCHONING (*resigned*). I knew it.

LULU. I'll fight!

SCHONING. Mignon . . .

LULU. How can you *change* like this?

SCHONING. It had to happen sooner or later.

LULU. I won't let you! I don't care if the whole world knocks me down and tramples on me. But not you. You've given me everything! You know me better than anyone else. You know you do!

SCHONING. If you want to show your gratitude, now is the time.

LULU. But not like this! Not like this!

SCHWARZ *comes in*.

SCHWARZ. What's happening?

LULU. He's trying to get rid of me.

SCHONING. Be quiet!

LULU. I'm the best! He's told me a thousand times!

SCHWARZ. Get out!

He grabs her by the arm and leads her out.

SCHONING (*alone*). It's Judgment Day.

SCHWARZ *returns*.

SCHWARZ. You'd better explain.

SCHONING. Shall we sit down?

SCHWARZ *sits*.

SCHWARZ. What did she mean?

SCHONING. You heard what she said.

SCHWARZ. Of course. She said that . . .

Thinks.

No, I didn't.

SCHONING. Perhaps because you didn't want to?

SCHWARZ. What do you mean?

SCHONING. Think of it as a business transaction. You were poor. She was rich . . .

SCHWARZ. I know.

SCHONING. Her husband never left you alone with her. Till I took pity on you, and dragged him away to see my son's rehearsal.

SCHWARZ. Yes?

SCHONING. Well, there you are. You married half a million marks.

SCHWARZ. And?

SCHONING. You have the art-world at your feet.

SCHWARZ. What about it?

SCHONING. When she met you, you were penniless and obscure!

SCHWARZ. You said that. I'm confused. Is she dissatisfied with me?

SCHONING. That's not the problem.

SCHWARZ. I'm a faithful husband. I support her. She has whatever a wife could want. What's she complaining about?

SCHONING. She isn't complaining.

SCHWARZ. Then what did she mean . . . you're trying to get rid of her?

SCHONING. She meant what she said.

SCHWARZ *goes pale*.

SCHWARZ. You mean she wants to . . . ?

SCHONING. You married half a million marks.

SCHWARZ. No, listen. Does she want to . . . be *unfaithful* to me?

SCHONING. Don't take it to heart. What's happened has happened.

SCHWARZ. *Happened*?

SCHONING. The fault is partly yours. If only . . .

SCHWARZ. *What's* happened?

SCHONING. She's just told you.

SCHWARZ. Her and . . . ? *You? What?*

He looks round the room in dawning comprehension.

Here in this room? This afternoon?

SCHONING. No, certainly not.

SCHWARZ. Thank God!

SCHONING. I've known your wife for fifteen years.

SCHWARZ. *How long?*

SCHONING. Before you take that sanctimonious tone, may I suggest that . . .

SCHWARZ. *Fifteen years?* But she's only . . .

SCHONING. You've done very well out of her. Look around you. Look at yourself. Commissioned up to your ears. All thanks to me. You're wealthy . . .

SCHWARZ. You've been betraying me all this time!

SCHONING. Fine. Let's shoot each other.

SCHWARZ. What?

SCHONING. Nobody lied to you.

SCHWARZ. No, that doesn't make sense. You said . . .

SCHONING. I came to your house today to end the affair.

SCHWARZ *is trying to get things straight in his head.*

SCHWARZ. The . . . *What? Fifteen years*? How old did you say she was when . . . ? When . . . ?

SCHONING. She was young. She was what's tactfully called a flower-seller. Barefoot. Selling her wares at café-tables.

SCHWARZ. She told me she was brought up by her cruel aunt.

SCHONING. That's the woman I lodged her with. I'm telling you this so that you won't imagine she's depraved by nature. It's her background. She was *taught* depravity.

SCHWARZ. She said that . . . when she married Dr. Goll . . . she was still a virgin. She swore it on her mother's grave.

SCHONING. She never knew her mother. She certainly never knew her grave. I very much doubt her mother *has* a grave.

SCHWARZ. How did she come to be married to Dr. Goll?

SCHONING. I passed her on. She was a favour between friends.

SCHWARZ. She said he never touched her.

SCHONING. They were married. Work it out for yourself.

SCHWARZ. She said that, when she married *me*, she was still a virgin.

SCHONING. What does it matter? Why were you chasing virgins anyway?

SCHWARZ. If she lied about that, I want nothing to do with her.

SCHONING. Don't demean yourself like this. It's sheer humiliation. Forget her past.

SCHWARZ. What *past*?

SCHONING. What do you think I'm trying to tell you? I'm talking about the slut that she used to be. And the slut that nobody'd guess she'd been, if they looked at her now. So what are you fussing about?

SCHWARZ. Eve?

SCHONING. I called her Mignon.

SCHWARZ. I thought her name was Popsy.

SCHONING. Only according to Dr. Goll. What her original name might be, I've no idea. Bearing in mind the character of her father . . . who is still, by the way, pursuing her . . .

SCHWARZ. Is he still alive?

SCHONING. I saw him today.

SCHWARZ. Where?

SCHONING. Here.

SCHWARZ. *Here?*

SCHONING. In this drawing-room. That's his glass.

SCHWARZ *looks at it, astonished.*

SCHWARZ. She told me he'd been carried away by a typhoon in the Philippines.

He grips his chest.

SCHONING. What is it?

SCHWARZ. I'm hurting.

SCHONING. A glass of water?

SCHWARZ *rises and staggers across the room.*

SCHWARZ. I can't breathe . . . if I could only scream.

SCHONING. Don't take it like this. You've not lost anything. She's still yours. And if you were happy once . . .

SCHWARZ. I was, I was . . .

SCHONING. Let's not be too judgmental. None of us is perfect. We all prostitute our talents in one way or other.

LULU *comes back in.*

LULU. Edvard . . .

SCHWARZ. Let me go.

He detaches himself and goes out.

SCHONING. Now the triangular finale.

LULU. What are you talking about?

SCHONING. He'll come back. He'll stamp his foot. I shall apologise. You will dissolve in tears. All three of us will perform our allotted roles, regardless of their unoriginal nature.

A noise from behind the door SCHWARZ *exited through.*

What's that?

Terrible and macabre groans are heard. SCHONING *rushes to the door and finds it locked.*

SCHONING. Open up at once!

LULU. He's trying to frighten us.

SCHONING. We'll have to break the door down. Get me an axe.

LULU. An *axe*?

The doorbell rings.

SCHONING. Who's that?

LULU. I'm not expecting anyone.

SCHONING. Say you're out.

LULU. It might be somebody wanting to buy a painting.

SCHONING. We just won't answer.

LULU *goes towards the door.*

Don't move! They'll hear you!

The door opens and ALWA *enters.*

ALWA. Father!

SCHONING. What are you doing here?

ALWA. The Government's collapsed.

SCHONING. Don't bother me now.

ALWA looks at LULU.

ALWA. What's happening?

SCHONING. I'll tell you in a moment.

SCHONING goes to the door and rattles it.

SCHONING. Schwarz! Schwarz!

ALWA. Would somebody like to explain all this?

A terrible rattle is heard from within.

Jesus!

SCHONING shouts at LULU:

SCHONING. Get me an axe!

LULU goes out.

ALWA. Did he catch you at it?

SCHONING. He worked it out. He couldn't face it. Fool that he is.

ALWA. I rather like him.

SCHONING. What did you say just now? The Government's collapsed?

ALWA. It certainly has.They're screaming for you down at the paper. Nobody knows what line to take.

SCHONING. Damn. Damn.

He calls through the keyhole:

Schwarz? Are you all right?

LULU comes back with an axe.

ALWA. Give me that.

He takes the axe. Whacks it against the door, doing considerable damage.

LULU. God help us. God help us all.

SCHONING (*to* ALWA, *of the axe*). Both hands, and further down the handle.

ALWA. Shut up, father!

The door flies open, revealing bloody walls. ALWA *peeps into the room, then staggers back, devastated.* LULU*'s knees give way and she collapses.*

Jesus Christ!

LULU (*to* SCHONING). You did that.

SCHONING. Be quiet!

He wipes his brow, braces himself and enters the room.

ALWA. Oh Jesus.

LULU. He must have tipped his head back.

She demonstrates.

Like that.

SCHONING *comes back from the suicide-room, flecked with blood and looking very green. There's a bell on* SCHWARZ*'s desk.* SCHONING *rings it.*

ALWA. I can't move. My legs are paralysed.

LULU. Hold my hand.

HENRIETTA, *the maid, comes in.*

HENRIETTA. Did somebody ring, sir?

SCHONING. I did. Do you by any chance know the name of Herr Schwarz's doctor?

HENRIETTA. That would be Dr. Bernstein, sir. He lives next door.

SCHONING. If he could spare a moment of his time, I would be most grateful.

HENRIETTA. Certainly sir. Is Herr Schwarz not feeling . . . ?

SCHONING. Quick as you can.

HENRIETTA. Quite so, sir.

She goes out.

ALWA. I cannot resist just one more look.

SCHONING. You disgust me. Indulge your appetite for drama in the appropriate place.

LULU. My heart's banging like a drum.

She starts to cry.

ALWA. My legs are shaking.

SCHONING. I tried to help him. And this is the thanks I get.

LULU (*to* ALWA). What's he talking about now?

ALWA. He thinks his marriage has been jeopardised.

SCHONING. *Jeopardised*? It's doomed. It's out of the question. Look at that room. That corpse. It's a front-page story.

ALWA. You're the newspaper editor. Write his obituary. That'll put them off the scent.

SCHONING. What would I say?

ALWA. 'He was depressed.'?

SCHONING. 'Depressed'? Yes, that might work. 'His art sprang newly-minted from the well-springs of his private agony.' What do we tell the police?

ALWA. Don't ask me. I've reached the limit of my advice. Your marriage is a damn nuisance as far as I'm concerned. You'll change your will and I'll have toddlers yapping round my ankles. (*Of* LULU.) Why don't you marry your tart? At least she won't be popping babies.

LULU. How do you know?

ALWA. I'll get it in writing.

SCHONING. Marry her yourself! I wash my hands of her.

He goes to the desk, gets paper and a pen, starts to write.

ALWA. Thank you, father. I'm not that desperate.

LULU (*to* ALWA). I wouldn't have you on my deathbed.

ALWA. Sadly still a hypothetical location.

SCHONING. I can hardly hold the pen. My hands are shaking.

ALWA. Apocalypse has commenced! I love it! *And* the Government's collapsed.

SCHONING. That's hardly top of my agenda.

ALWA. So you say. Your newsroom's like a madhouse. Shouldn't you be there?

SCHONING. I'm writing.

ALWA. One more look.

He goes to the door and looks into the blood-boltered room. SCHONING *writes:*

SCHONING. 'The price of genius is a tragic instability . . . '

LULU (*to* SCHONING). You've got blood on you. Don't move. I'll wipe it off.

She does, as far as possible.

You'll have to marry me now.

SCHONING. Marry a whore?

He laughs. Goes on writing.

LULU. Don't laugh. You're in trouble.

SCHONING. I can handle it.

LULU. Not on your own, you can't. You'll need me to back your story up when the police arrive.

SCHONING. You will.

LULU. Don't count on it.

SCHONING *stops writing. Stares at her.*

SCHONING. You're appalling.

LULU. Say it again.

SCHONING. You're vile.

LULU. Try harder.

SCHONING. Are you angel or devil?

LULU. I'm neither. This is me. I've never pretended to be anything else. All the rest is just your imagination. You think about that.

She takes away the piece of paper he's writing on.

Shall I do you a dance while you're thinking? What would you like? The Teddy-bear Tango? The Milkmaid Minuet? Why don't you get your whip out? No, I've a better idea.

She gives him a new piece of paper and puts the pen in his hand.

Write a letter.

SCHONING. Now?

LULU. Yes, now. Write what I tell you. To the daughter of the Baroness zum Bergen. 'Dear Fräulein . . . '

He hesitates.

Do it!

SCHONING. I call her Adelaide.

LULU. 'Dear *Fräulein*'. Go on.

He starts to write.

'I must withdraw my offer of marriage. I cannot reconcile your innocence with my own corruption.'

SCHONING. I can't write this.

LULU. Shall I send for the police?

He writes.

'I write to you at the command of the woman who controls my life. Who is my master.'

He writes. The door opens and HENRIETTA *shows in* DR. BERNSTEIN. *He's a kindly Jewish doctor, expecting to deal with a mild bout of flu.*

HENRIETTA. Doctor Bernstein has arrived.

LULU *indicates the door.*

LULU. My husband's in there.

DR. BERNSTEIN. May I ask what the problem is?

LULU. Depression.

DR. BERNSTEIN. Ah! Depression.

He smiles: depression he can deal with. He goes towards the door, as:

End of Act Two.

ACT THREE

A grand hall in German renaissance style, with a ceiling of carved oak. The lower half of the wall is dark carved wood, the upper half hung with Gobelins tapestries. At opposite sides of the hall are two portières, i.e. curtained doorways or entrances.

A monumental staircase descends from a curtained gallery. LULU's Pierrot portrait is prominently displayed, now in a gold frame.

Around and about are antiquities, oriental objets d'art, pieces of armour, animal skins. On a square oak table is a porcelain vase, painted with flamingos and filled with white flowers.

COUNTESS GESCHWITZ sits on an ottoman. Her hands are hidden in her muff. LULU is there. SCHONING stands apart from the two women.

GESCHWITZ. You cannot imagine, Dr. Schoning, how much I look forward to seeing your wife at the Ladies' Arts Ball.

SCHONING. I hope her costume won't be too indelicate.

GESCHWITZ. Have no fear! Frau Schoning's taste is far too refined for that.

SCHONING. Since men are barred from the Ball, I'll never find out.

LULU. I'm only going because the Countess asked me. I'd be just as happy not to.

SCHONING. But may I really not attend?

GESCHWITZ. It's out of the question, Dr. Schoning! Even the merest hint of the male animal would ruin the evening.

SCHONING. Isn't that taking exclusivity to extremes?

GESCHWITZ. Exclusivity is the very essence of our annual
  Ball. It would be abject treachery to betray it. Our ladies
  have opportunity enough to dance with men on other
  occasions. At the Ladies' Ball, they belong to us.

SCHONING. We men would be no serious competition,
  surely? What if one came in some all-enveloping disguise?

GESCHWITZ. We are adamant.

SCHONING. I'm no threat, I can assure you.

  He takes out a cigarette-case.

  Do the ladies smoke?

GESCHWITZ. I will, if I may.

  She takes a cigarette.

SCHONING. Mignon?

LULU. No thank you.

GESCHWITZ (*to* LULU). Do you never indulge?

LULU. Not for pleasure.

SCHONING. Frau Schoning smokes for appearance only.

LULU. May I offer you a liqueur, Countess?

GESCHWITZ. Don't trouble yourself for me.

LULU. Oh, it's no trouble.

  A bottle and glasses have been laid out. LULU *pours two
  glasses.* SCHONING *sniffs the flowers.*

SCHONING. Tuber-roses. Exquisite.

LULU. They're my present from the Countess.

SCHONING (*to* GESCHWITZ). You'll be destitute at this rate.
  (*To* LULU.) But it isn't your birthday, is it?

LULU. I've been wondering that myself.

SCHONING. Virginal white. A curious choice of colour.

LULU. I don't understand the language of flowers.

GESCHWITZ. These were the only flowers they had in the shop.

LULU (*to* SCHONING). You see? Now stop being nasty.

She and GESCHWITZ *raise their glasses.* LULU *knocks back her drink.* GESCHWITZ *takes a sip. Her gaze alights on* LULU's *portrait.*

GESCHWITZ. How pretty you are. Quite lovely. In that portrait, I mean.

They all look at it.

I would adore to see you dressed like that, just once. Who is the artist?

LULU. His name was Edvard Schwarz.

GESCHWITZ. Is he no longer alive?

SCHONING. He cut his throat.

LULU (*to* GESCHWITZ). Ignore him. (*To* SCHONING.) You're in a filthy mood.

GESCHWITZ. If the painter was in love with you, I can imagine that he might be driven to . . . no, I shouldn't say it.

LULU. He was fated.

GESCHWITZ. Who isn't? I must leave you now. I have a life-class to attend this evening. And there's still so much to prepare for the Ladies' Ball.

RODRIGO, an acrobat, looks out from one of the portières. He wears a brightly-checked, buttoned-up suit with bell-bottomed trousers, somewhat short. Crimson cravat, single gold earring. He hovers, watching.

SCHONING. Must I give up hope entirely? Couldn't I watch unseen from one of the boxes?

GESCHWITZ. Good. Day. Doctor. Schoning.

LULU. Thank you for calling, Countess.

RODRIGO pops back without being noticed. LULU *shows the Countess out, leaving* SCHONING *alone, as far as he is aware.*

SCHONING. My wife seduced by a degenerate woman!

He looks at the flowers.

These are the proof.

He looks around at various nooks and crannies.

I can tolerate the scandal. I can brave that out. The laughter behind my back. The jeers. The scorn. But that my home should be polluted! She'll soon be back. I'll wait. I'll catch them *in flagrante*. Then I'll strike. With all my moral and physical strength. What's left of it.

LULU *comes back.*

LULU. She kissed my hand like a man.

SCHONING. Will you try your new costume on for me tonight?

LULU. No.

SCHONING. Although next week you'll flaunt it to a ballroom-full of strangers.

LULU. You're not a stranger.

SCHONING. I'd simply like to see it before . . .

LULU. It isn't for men to look at. It's for women.

SCHONING. Just for women.

He starts to go.

LULU. Where are you going?

SCHONING. I have a newspaper to run.

LULU. You're never at home these days.

SCHONING. I have no choice. Supporting you and your string of admirers costs me more than the Duke of Sheffield spends on his five racing stallions.

LULU. I'd rather die than be as miserable as you are.

SCHONING. You make dying sound almost pleasant.

LULU. Perhaps it is.

SCHONING. Those who live for pleasure, die for pleasure.

LULU. I want to live for pleasure first.

SCHONING. And when the pleasure grows too hard to bear . .
. You were supposed to make life easy. That's why I married
you.

LULU. Except you didn't.

SCHONING. What did I do?

LULU. I married you.

SCHONING. A risky step.

*He kisses her on the forehead. Opens a jewel-encrusted box.
Takes out two surgical phials, one small, one large. He slips
the larger one into his breast pocket. Undoes his cufflinks,
rolls up his sleeve slightly. Meanwhile, to LULU:*

What did the Countess want?

LULU. She wants to paint me. She's an unusual woman.

SCHONING. Oh, she is.

*With a hypodermic, SCHONING shoots up the contents of
the smaller phial.*

LULU. She gives me a prickle all down my back. It's like
seeing a ghost. Don't do that.

SCHONING. My hands are shaking.

LULU. You promised you wouldn't.

SCHONING. I tried to stop.

LULU. Can't you get drunk instead?

*SCHONING rolls back his sleeve, does up his cuff-links.
Breathes out heavily.*

SCHONING. I'm dining out.

LULU embraces and kisses him. He frees himself.

Not now, not now. A respectable girl like you. I'll see you
tonight.

He goes. RODRIGO *sticks his head out from behind the portière:*

RODRIGO. Can I . . . ?

LULU. Ssh! Get back!

RODRIGO. You asked me round for a drink. And I've been hiding in here since noon . . .

LULU. All right. Come out for a moment.

He comes out.

RODRIGO. Here, Mitzi. What would you say to a quick . . . ?

LULU. Not now. Here's your drink.

She hands him a filled glass. He knocks it back. Stretches a leg.

RODRIGO. It's cramped in there.

LULU. I thought you were a contortionist.

RODRIGO. I'm an acrobat, mainly. What about later?

LULU. Maybe. Probably. God, those muscles.

She feels them.

RODRIGO. What are the chances of that fifty marks you mentioned?

LULU. What for?

RODRIGO. Services rendered.

He puts an arm round her waist. She pushes it off.

LULU. Hands off. Not here.

RODRIGO. Then might I suggest a more convenient place? The café 'Lorelei' would be perfect. None of this hide-and seek one gets in private houses. Spotless rooms, clean linen . . .

LULU. Get in. He's coming back.

RODRIGO. Forty marks?

LULU. He's got a gun.

RODRIGO. Twenty?

A door is heard. Footsteps.

LULU. Do you want him to shoot you?

RODRIGO *disappears behind the portière.* LULU *checks the curtain is closed.*

LULU. I thought he'd never go.

ALWA *appears in the doorway, very smartly-dressed as though for a society occasion, top hat in hand.*

ALWA. I saw my father on the doorstep.

LULU. Where is he now?

ALWA. He's gone at last. He never could exit cleanly. What's the matter?

LULU. I'm upset. I wish I was hundreds of miles away.

ALWA. Away from me?

LULU. No, not from you. You're the only person I can talk to. Your father's been grinding his teeth all day. He hates me.

ALWA. I'm not worried. I'm not even jealous. He can have you whenever he likes. You'll still be mine.

He sits her down.

I feel it everywhere I go. When I'm out riding. When I'm drinking. When I'm lolling about on a sofa. I can feel you. I can feel your body.

He makes a grab at her.

LULU. Not yet! Be nice to me first. Do something about the pain I'm feeling.

ALWA *glances towards the portière behind which* RODRIGO *is hiding.*

ALWA. What's that noise?

LULU. There's nobody here.

ALWA. Aren't you well?

LULU. I'm fine. I haven't made love for the last two weeks.
I don't know why. You're looking handsome.

ALWA. Top hat, white gloves.

LULU. I want to make love to you dressed like this. Then die.
Supper's arranged.

ALWA. You didn't just promise me supper. You said an orgy.
Isn't that right? An orgy for two. I've been thinking about it
all day. Every time the cab bumped over a pebble, I thought
I was going to explode. And here you are! I can see your
knees underneath your dress. The sway of your hips. Your
eyes. If we don't do something soon, I swear I'll turn into
a sex-murderer.

LULU. One of these days I'd like to be murdered.

ALWA. What did the Countess want?

LULU. Me.

She laughs.

I couldn't understand it at first, but . . .

As she continues, SCHONING *appears on the gallery
above. He pulls a curtain slightly aside and watches.*

. . . then, this morning, when I got out of the bath, I looked
at myself in the mirror . . . and I pulled my hair up into a
knot . . .

She shows him.

. . . like this . . .

SCHONING. My own son!

LULU . . . . and I suddenly saw what she meant. I thought, I'd
like to open my legs and get between them. I thought I'd
love to be a man for a change, a man who belonged to me
and nobody else . . .

ALWA. Oh!

LULU. I wouldn't want to be a man for any other reason.
When you're a woman, you can be kissed all over your
body . . .

ALWA insinuates his head into her lap.

ALWA. Katya! Katya!

LULU. Mmm.

ALWA. I can feel your flesh . . . no blouse . . . no corsets . . .
just you . . . you . . .

He feels further.

. . . in silk that clings to every mound and hollow . . .

*He's suddenly shocked and surprised by what his hands
have encountered.*

What's that?

LULU. This is for you.

*She draws away from him, stands and slips off her tea-
gown. She's wearing, underneath it, her Ladies' Ball
costume. It's amazingly exotic and sexy. ALWA falls to the
floor and presses LULU's feet to his lips.*

It's what I'll wear to the Ball next week. Do you like it?

*In the gallery, SCHONING lets the curtain fall and sinks
from view.*

ALWA. I can't look at it . . . you've seen into my heart . . . my
bones . . . Oh Katya!

LULU pulls her foot away.

. . . these ankles . . . toes . . . the capriccio of the knees . . .
the andante of the thighs . . . it's like a choir of children's
voices . . . I can aspire no higher!

LULU. Don't . . . not yet.

*She rings a bell. ALWA sits at the table and collapses.
LULU sits opposite him. RODRIGO, behind ALWA's back,
pops out of the portière to look at the costume. LULU, with
a furious glance, shoos him back. Meanwhile FERDINAND,*

a servant, enters and lays the table: cold partridge pâté and a bottle of Pommery on ice.

LULU. Do you approve the year? Taste it.

ALWA tastes the wine. Nods. FERDINAND throws the napkin over his arm and leaves.

LULU. Don't worry about him. He's very discreet.

ALWA fills their glasses.

ALWA. I feel like a soul that rubs its eyes and finds it's woken up in heaven.

LULU. I feel like a butterfly which has burst from its chrysalis.

ALWA. The sparkle in your eyes is like a well that somebody's dropped a pebble into.

LULU (*of his tie*). How many tries did it take to get that bow so perfect?

ALWA. I got it in one.

He fills the glasses once more. Both are silent for a few moments. LULU passes ALWA a truffle from her own plate.

LULU. I never could love a man who was badly dressed.

ALWA. What if he wore . . .

LULU. Tell me.

ALWA . . . . leather shorts . . . and a shirt of patent fibre . . . and a medal around his neck.

LULU. I'd rather strangle him than watch him take them off.

ALWA. Oh Katya!

He rings the bell. FERDINAND enters with a plate of asparagus. He serves them.

(*Annoyed, to* FERDINAND.) Are you perspiring?

FERDINAND. Hardly at all, sir.

LULU. Leave him alone.

FERDINAND. One's only human.

ALWA. Bring us another bottle.

FERDINAND. Very good, sir.

He takes away what's left of the partridge pâté.
SCHONING reappears on the gallery and watches. He has
a revolver.

ALWA. I'm waking up. Hand me your plate.

LULU passes him her plate. She fills their glasses. ALWA
serves the asparagus.

After our supper, I shall address a subject which is dear to
us both.

LULU. I wait with interest.

ALWA. My tongue may touch on a sensitive area.

LULU. Ah.

ALWA. If you'll allow it.

LULU. I'll allow it.

ALWA. It will dart and flicker.

LULU. My lips will quiver with excitement.

ALWA. You'll grab me by the hair . . . !

They laugh.

LULU. I want to be here, like this, for the rest of my life.

ALWA. I'm seeing you now as though I'd never seen you
before. Your fingers round the asparagus-stalk. Your tongue
. . . against it.

LULU takes a stalk of asparagus out of her mouth.

LULU. It's soft.

ALWA. It's stiffening.

LULU. Eat!

ALWA. I can't.

He gets up.

One kiss . . .

LULU. Get back!

She stretches her hand across the table. ALWA kisses it, concentrating on the cleft between two fingers.

ALWA. It's wet.

LULU. There's butter on it.

ALWA *sinks to the floor, places her bare arm over his head and kisses her armpit.*

ALWA. Caviar! Caviar!

LULU *fills his glass.*

LULU. Wash it down.

She wipes her finger on the napkin.

There's more to come.

She rings.

ALWA. Three dozen oysters would be bread and milk compared to the feast I'm planning.

FERDINAND *comes on, changes the dishes, serves roast quails aux champignons and produces two more bottles of Pommery, uncorking one.*

FERDINAND. Coffee is ready.

LULU (*to* ALWA). Shall we drink it on the patio?

ALWA (*to* FERDINAND). You can serve it in the bedroom.

FERDINAND. Certainly, sir. And what will it be to accompany, Frau Schoning? Whisky, brandy, curaçao . . . ?

ALWA. He's very nervous for a butler.

FERDINAND. That's true, sir. I'm not used to table duties.

ALWA. Life's a journey of discovery.

LULU. Leave him alone! You're bullying him!

FERDINAND. I am the coachman, sir. I only go into Madame's bedroom by invitation.

SCHONING. My God, him too!

> FERDINAND *goes.* ALWA *tears a quail apart. Eats it messily. Looks at* LULU.

ALWA. You keep your distance . . . you perfume the moment . . . you surround the delights to come with food . . . and scent . . . and flesh . . . it's Machiavellian . . . but your . . .

> LULU *lies back, extends her arms.*

LULU. What?

ALWA. Your what?

LULU. My . . .

> RODRIGO *pops out from his portière. Stares.* SCHONING *sees him.*

SCHONING. Christ! There's another one!

> RODRIGO *pops back. Meanwhile:*

LULU. Come to the Ladies' Ball with me. I'll smuggle you in. Those women are after me like rutting foxes.

ALWA (*of the vegetable in his hand*). What's this?

LULU. A stick of celery.

> ALWA *throws it in the air.*

ALWA. I can't endure this any longer! If you've a spark of soul left in your body! Pity me!

> *He sinks to the floor, embraces* LULU's *knee.*

Let me die!

> LULU *lets his head slip between her knees. Touches his forehead.*

LULU. You're hot.

ALWA. Let me be your martyr. You whore. You spunk-hole. You blood-cloth. You arse-wipe. You piss-pot. You wank-rag.

> LULU, *looks up and sees* SCHONING *looking down on them. Their eyes meet.*

LULU. This is the most beautiful moment of my life.

SCHONING starts to descend the stairs, revolver in hand.
ALWA looks up and sees him.

ALWA. Father!

SCHONING. Out!

ALWA. Don't be ridiculous.

SCHONING. Do you want me to shoot you?

ALWA. Hooray! Hooray! Authority speaks! The Marquis of
Droop!

SCHONING. I will!

LULU. He won't.

SCHONING. Out! Out!

He grabs ALWA by the collar and pulls him out of the door.
RODRIGO dashes out from behind the portière and starts
up the stairs. LULU blocks his path.

LULU. Where do you think you're going?

RODRIGO. I'm getting out!

LULU. Don't leave me!

RODRIGO. Move!

LULU. Too late! He's coming back!

RODRIGO (*of the portière*). I'm not going back there. I can't
even see which way he's pointing the gun.

LULU. Hide!

RODRIGO backs into the room.

RODRIGO. Oh hell, oh bugger it. What have I done to deserve
this?

SCHONING is heard approaching. RODRIGO dives under
the tablecloth. SCHONING comes in. He advances, gun at
the ready, towards the portière, and throws the curtain
aside. To LULU:

SCHONING. Where's the other one gone?

LULU. Through the window.

SCHONING. Through the window?

LULU. He's an acrobat.

SCHONING *locks the door. While his back is turned,*
RODRIGO *starts to emerge from under the tablecloth,*
thinks better of it and goes back under it.

SCHONING (*to* LULU). Let me look at you in your costume.

LULU. Haven't you seen enough?

SCHONING. You look incredible.

LULU. Don't I?

SCHONING. As though you've from come a different world.
Beyond the sunset.

LULU. I designed it myself.

SCHONING. What is it meant to be? Some kind of . . . tight-
rope walker?

LULU. An earth-spirit.

SCHONING. If it weren't for your baby eyes, the way it
shows your hips would be a public scandal.

LULU. It's better than keeping them hidden away.

SCHONING. Did you plan to attend the Ladies Arts Ball like
that?

LULU. I did.

SCHONING. Without an ounce of shame?

LULU. They'll mob me.

SCHONING. I'm just an old fool.

LULU. You are.

SCHONING *leads her to the ottoman.*

What do you want?

SCHONING. I want to rattle my bones into life. Just one last time.

LULU. Get rid of that gun.

SCHONING. It's not in the way.

LULU *is on his knees.*

LULU. Give it to me.

SCHONING. I will. That's why I brought it.

He puts the revolver in her hand. She stretches up her arm and shoots at the ceiling.

They're not blanks, by the way.

LULU *takes a closer look at the revolver.*

LULU. What do you want me to do with it?

SCHONING. I want you to shoot yourself.

LULU *stands. Adjusts her blouse.*

LULU. If you wanted to punish me, you should have brought your whip.

SCHONING. That's schoolboy stuff.

LULU. Oh, I don't know. It might give you a few ideas.

SCHONING *puts his arms around her waist.*

SCHONING. Kiss me.

She sinks on his knees, throws her arms around his neck, kisses him.

LULU. Let's get rid of the gun.

SCHONING. Those lips. They're softer by the day.

LULU. Let's put it away somewhere.

SCHONING. You'll need it.

LULU *kisses him.*

LULU. Shoot me yourself.

SCHONING. I'd go to prison.

LULU. That's not the reason. You haven't the heart.

SCHONING. Aim it at yours. If you can find it.

She does.

LULU. It's warm.

SCHONING. Now pull the trigger.

She tries a few times with no result.

You're not trying.

She drops the revolver.

LULU. Ah!

SCHONING. My fault.

She leans her head back and rubs her knees together. Yawns.

LULU. My legs have gone to sleep.

SCHONING. Sweet rivals.

LULU. Who calls them that?

SCHONING. I do. When I look at them. Snuggled up side by side, each one thinking the other one's prettier.

She stretches out her feet.

LULU. Do you want to tie them up?

SCHONING. I ought to. When you lie back . . .

LULU . . . . they jump apart . . .

SCHONING . . . . like angry lovers.

LULU. You could tie me up and beat me. Till I bled. I wouldn't scream. I'd bite on my handkerchief.

SCHONING. There'd be no point.

LULU. Then you'll just have to forgive me.

SCHONING. I did that long ago. Give me your hand.

He guides her hand so that the gun is pointing at her breast.

Keep calm.

She cries.

LULU. I'm so happy. Why should I die, when I'm happy like this? I've only done the same as everyone else. I'm a woman. I'm a woman. I'm young.

SCHONING. Damn!

He pushes her off his knee and stands. Walks angrily away. LULU lies on the ottoman, the revolver against her breast, weeping.

LULU. I can't. I can't. Be patient with me. I can't do it.

She falls to the ground, sinks her head on the floor.

I can't think. Everything's gone black.

SCHONING *is suddenly uncertain.*

SCHONING. Should I . . . ? Should I do it myself?

LULU. No . . . no!

RODRIGO *leaps out from under the table and grabs SCHONING by the arm.*

RODRIGO. Look out!

SCHONING *spins round.* LULU *shoots him twice. One of the bullets hits* RODRIGO*'s left hand.*

Shit!

SCHONING *falls forward to the ground.* ALWA *appears on the gallery.* RODRIGO, *his hand streaming with blood, leads* SCHONING *to the ottoman.*

(*To* LULU.) You got my hand.

LULU *approaches* SCHONING.

LULU. Did I hurt you?

SCHONING. You must leave the country. Get to safety. Take my keys . . . they're in my pocket . . . in my desk . . . are

sixty thousand marks . . . quick as you can . . . get me some
water . . . a glass of water . . . Earth-spirit!

RODRIGO. Champagne, sir?

SCHONING. Yes, champagne.

RODRIGO *pours a glass from the open bottle of
champagne.*

I'm thirsty.

LULU. Let me.

She kneels and raises the glass to SCHONING'*s lips.*

SCHONING. Little murderess.

RODRIGO *opens the other bottle of champagne.*

RODRIGO. Have as much as you like.

ALWA *approaches* SCHONING.

SCHONING. 'Et tu, Brute,' Alwa. You'll be next.

RODRIGO *offers him another glass.*

RODRIGO. Here, sir. Get this down you.

SCHONING. There's blood in it.

RODRIGO. It's only mine, sir.

SCHONING. I'm dreaming.

RODRIGO. Won't harm you.

LULU (*to* RODRIGO). I wasn't aiming at you.

RODRIGO (*binding his hand*). Forget it.

SCHONING. So you're . . . an acrobat?

RODRIGO. And a contortionist, sir.

To LULU, *of the drink she's pouring.*

Don't be stingy.

SCHONING. I'm feeling better.

ALWA. Shouldn't somebody send for a doctor?

SCHONING. Take the keys . . . I can't move . . . you'll need the money . . . my mother used to travel every summer . . . summer month . . .

LULU *kisses him*.

LULU. Look at us!

SCHONING . . . . month . . . morphine . . .

RODRIGO. Give him a drop more.

SCHONING. Don't bother about the doctor . . . over the bridge . . . kiss me . . .

LULU *kisses him and lays her right hand on his heart*.

RODRIGO. He gets the kisses. All I'll get is a last cigarette.

ALWA. Who are you?

RODRIGO. I'm an acrobat, sir.

ALWA (*nods in comprehension*). Ah.

LULU *stands*.

LULU. He's dead.

ALWA *gets down, starts emptying* SCHONING's *pockets*.

ALWA. We'll put the revolver in his hand. Before it stiffens.

RODRIGO. That won't help, sir. Not in a court of law. He can't very well have shot himself in the back.

SCHONING. Over the bridge!

ALWA *springs back in a fright*.

ALWA. Jesus! He's alive!

LULU *takes a close look at* SCHONING.

LULU. He's gone now. Give me my dress. He's lying on it.

ALWA *gets her morning dress from under* SCHONING *and throws it to* LULU.

I'm leaving.

ALWA. Take me with you.

LULU (*of the dress*). It's covered in blood.

ALWA *holds up a bunch of keys.*

ALWA. I've got the key to his desk. If you don't take me with you, then you'll never see the sixty thousand marks.

LULU. All right! Whatever you want!

ALWA *rushes to the desk. A curtain is pulled aside in the gallery and* SCHIGOLCH *appears. He sniffs the air.*

SCHIGOLCH. Who's been firing guns in here?

ALWA. Who's that?

LULU. My father. What are you waiting for? Go and open the desk!

SCHIGOLCH (*to* ALWA). You heard what she said, young man.

RODRIGO. We can empty the safe as well.

SCHIGOLCH. And lock up the house.

LULU (*to* ALWA). Hurry up! There's a train at eight!

ALWA. But where are we going?

LULU. To Paris of course.

ALWA / SCHIGOLCH / RODRIGO. To Paris!

End of Act Three.

ACT FOUR

*Paris. A spacious drawing-room in white stucco. Double door
in the back wall. A rococo console with a large mirror over it,
and other large mirrors mounted on the walls. A white marble
fireplace: over it,* LULU*'s Pierrot portrait.*

*In the drawing-room, moving about the room in lively
conversation, are* LULU, COUNTESS GESCHWITZ, ALWA
SCHONING *and* RODRIGO. *Also present:* MARQUIS
CASTI-PIANI, *the banker* PUNTSCHU, MADELEINE DE
MARELLE, *her thirteen-year-old daughter* KADEGA,
BIANETTA GAZIL *and* LUDMILA STEINHERZ. *Beyond the
centre doors can be seen a large baccarat-table.*

LULU *wears a white directoire gown with large sleeves and
lace falling down to her feet. Her gloves are white kid and her
hair is piled up high, topped with a plume of white feathers.*
GESCHWITZ *wears a pale-blue Hussar's jacket, trimmed with
silver braid, stiff cuffs with enormous cuff-links and a white
bow tie.*

BOB, LULU*'s groom, serves champagne. He is fourteen and
wears a red jacket, gleaming top-boots and bulging
lederhosen.*

RODRIGO *is proposing a toast:*

RODRIGO. Lords, ladies and gentlemen . . . Mesdames,
Messieurs . . . quiet please . . . if I may . . . what's the
French for 'Geburtstag'?

SEVERAL. 'Birthday'.

RODRIGO. Thank you. I wish to propose a toast to our
delightful hostess, whose 'birthday' we are here to
celebrate. To the Countess of Munich!

All raise their glasses to LULU.

ALWA. And many happy returns to my new and lovely wife. . . Katya!

He kisses her, to a spatter of appreciative applause.
RODRIGO, who has stepped down, chats to the women
beside him.

BIANETTA. We were admiring your athletic physique, Monsieur. Do you lift weights?

RODRIGO. It is my *métier*, ladies.

LUDMILA. My preference is for marksmen. I saw one at the Casino, not a week ago. I trembled every time he extended his arm and his pistol *cracked*.

BIANETTA. But look at the hands on this one! So graceful . . . and so enormous!

She puts her hand in RODRIGO's.

My own little paw has quite disappeared!

LUDMILA (*glancing at RODRIGO's hand*). How did you get that scar? Was it a shooting incident?

MADELEINE DE MARELLE *is in conversation with*
ALWA *and* PUNTSCHU.

PUNTSCHU. I wonder, Madame, that we have never before had the pleasure of meeting your charming daughter.

MADELEINE. Do you find her charming?

PUNTSCHU. Charming? She's a wonder! She's a pert little peach!

CASTI-PIANI. How old is she?

MADELEINE. Not quite thirteen. She's only here in Paris for the night. In the morning she must return to her convent.

PUNTSCHU. I would have taken her for older . . . she seems ripe for the picking!

KADEGA *approaches.*

KADEGA. Are you talking about me, Maman?

MADELEINE. I was just telling these gentlemen about your geometry prize.

PUNTSCHU. Look at the bloom on her skin!

CASTI-PIANI. Those tiny feet! That delicate trot!

PUNTSCHU. I'd pay you fifty louis, Madame, for the privilege of instructing this adorable child in the mysteries of the adult world.

MADELEINE. Not for a million francs!

She kisses KADEGA.

CASTI-PIANI. What would you say to a diamond necklace?

MADELEINE. Don't waste my time, dear Casti-Piani . . . you couldn't afford it.

To PUNTSCHU:

On the other hand, Monsieur Puntschu . . . do you have any more of the Jungfrau shares to spare?

PUNTSCHU. Several thousand. But I will not let them out of my grasp. In one week's time, those Jungfrau shares will be worth a fortune, mark my words.

MADELEINE. You'll be in trouble from me if they're not. I've sunk everything I've got in them.

ALWA. So have I. He'd better be right.

PUNTSCHU. Respected clients, allow me to reassure you. This time next year, you must go to Switzerland. Look at the Alps, watch the Jungfrau funicular railway twirling like a silvery snake between the mountains, and you'll bless me for the incredible wealth I've brought you.

MADELEINE. That's a relief!

LUDMILA *and* BIANETTA *pass by.*

LUDMILA. Aren't you playing?

BIANETTA. They're starting!

MADELEINE. Wait for me, Bianetta!

They move towards the gaming-room. PUNTSCHU *offers his arm to* LUDMILA.

PUNTSCHU. You be my partner! You have a lucky hand.

He takes her arm and they go. RODRIGO *approaches* GESCHWITZ, *who is sitting silently, watching* LULU.

RODRIGO. Countess? Shall we go in?

She shudders.

I'm not that frightening, am I?

GESCHWITZ. Get away.

RODRIGO. Would you like to feel my muscles?

GESCHWITZ. Out of my sight, you oaf!

BIANETTA, *on her way out, calls to* RODRIGO:

BIANETTA. This way, strongman!

RODRIGO. Wait for me, Bianetta!

LUDMILA. Aren't you joining us, Count Casti-Piani?

CASTI-PIANI. Go on ahead.

RODRIGO *leaves.* CASTI-PIANI *catches* LULU *on her way out.*

Sit down.

He turns to COUNTESS GESCHWITZ, *who is the only other guest left.*

You. Leave us.

LULU. Have I upset you?

CASTI-PIANI (*to* GESCHWITZ). Are you deaf?

With dignity, GESCHWITZ *goes into the gaming-room.*

LULU. What do you want from me?

CASTI-PIANI. You've nothing left to offer.

LULU. That's a horrible thing to say.

CASTI-PIANI. It's true. You've even given me your heart.

LULU. I only wish you weren't so rough with it.

CASTI-PIANI. People like you and me can't afford to have feelings.

LULU. You have no heart at all.

CASTI-PIANI. I do. It's small but vulnerable. It's my Achilles heel. When I see a woman in distress, it bleeds. Right now it's bleeding heavily.

LULU. What are you talking about?

CASTI-PIANI. Remorse. Betrayal. My Gethsemane.

LULU. Get to the point.

CASTI-PIANI. I know who you are. I know what happened to Dr. Schoning.

LULU. Dr . . . ?

CASTI-PIANI. I mean the third of your strikingly shortlived husbands. You're wanted for murder.

LULU. What are you?

CASTI-PIANI. Guess.

LULU. Are you a police informer?

CASTI-PIANI. I work for the German authorities. They, in turn, work closely with those here in France. If I were to grab you by the throat right now, and call for the police, they'd clap you in irons and send you home for trial.

LULU. They'll cut my head off!

CASTI-PIANI. True.

LULU. How can you do this?

CASTI-PIANI. I'll get a reward. Ten thousand francs. There's an alternative. Since my work for the police is not demanding, I've developed a business interest. It's an employment agency. I think you'll agree that the job I'm offering you is well suited to your natural talents.

LULU. You're making fun of me.

CASTI-PIANI. Not at all.

He takes an opened letter from his pocket.

This is a letter from one Epaminondas Oikonomopulos, the proprietor of a house in Cairo. I sent him your photographs . . .

LULU. Do you mean the photographs I gave you?

CASTI-PIANI. One of you as an Earth-spirit, one as Pierrot and one of you as Eve, I suppose, in front of a mirror. I had no use for them.

He hands her the letter.

Read it.

LULU. It's in English.

CASTI-PIANI. He offers me fifteen thousand francs. For you.

LULU. You bastard!

CASTI-PIANI. I've told him that you're skilled and experienced. Which is putting it mildly. Take my advice. Accept his offer and go to Cairo.

LULU. To a *brothel!*

CASTI-PIANI. The good thing about Egyptian brothels is that young ladies aren't hauled out to have their heads cut off. The clients, maybe.

LULU. I'd rather die. I'd rather have the skin torn off my back.

CASTI-PIANI. What're you complaining about? A brothel's your natural habitat. You'll be lucky to find a cosier one than this. It's got an exclusive clientèle. You'll work the hours that suit you . . . dress like a queen . . . lounge about your private bedroom, silken sheets and a view of minarets, I shouldn't wonder.

LULU. I've only got my body. It's all I am. Must I give it to any fat pig who wants it? Even if he's covered in hair like a baboon? With stinking breath? Is that what I've kept my innocence for?

CASTI-PIANI. I didn't get where I am by paying attention to the squeals of innocent victims.

LULU. Take me yourself! I'll do anything for you! You know I will!

CASTI-PIANI. The police are outside the house. Think it over. You can die five times a day on sheets of silk. Or once on the block in a German prison. I recommend the former.

He gets up.

LULU. Isn't there anything I can give you?

CASTI-PIANI. You told me yourself you'd nothing left.

LULU. I've got my Jungfrau shares.

CASTI-PIANI. I don't trust shares. Epaminondas Oikonomopulos pays in gold.

LULU. I could sell them. They're worth, oh, twelve or thirteen thousand. Give me three days.

CASTI-PIANI. I'll think about it.

He goes into the gaming room. LULU gets out her shares: they bear a highly-coloured picture of an Alpine sunset. She counts them feverishly. ALWA comes in from the gaming-room and she hurriedly puts them away.

ALWA. It's going brilliantly! Puntschu's upping the stakes. The madwoman's lost her shirt. Aren't you playing?

LULU. Why not?

He goes back into the gaming-room. LULU follows him only as far as the door, where she meets GESCHWITZ coming out.

GESCHWITZ. Are you going because of me?

LULU. I didn't see you.

GESCHWITZ. So you say. I need to speak with you.

She comes in, closing the door behind her.

You're destroying yourself. You've chosen the vilest, most degraded creature to be your lover . . .

LULU. Which one do you mean?

GESCHWITZ. Count Casti-Piani.

LULU. Be quiet, he'll hear you!

GESCHWITZ. He's vice incarnate.

LULU. Stop this!

GESCHWITZ. I've never seen a face so steeped in evil.

LULU *approaches her violently.*

LULU. Leave me alone!

GESCHWITZ. Go on! Hit me!

LULU *retreats.*

You scorn even to hit me.

LULU. I do.

GESCHWITZ. Listen to me. I beg you. If your feelings for me are not entirely . . . comparable to those that I have for you . . . at least remember that I've given up everything. All that I owned. My home, my wealth, my reputation. Free yourself from that abominable creature. Come to me.

LULU. Flee from bondage into bondage?

GESCHWITZ *slides to the floor.*

GESCHWITZ. I love you.

LULU. Leave me alone. I've got enough pain to deal with.

GESCHWITZ. Trample on me.

LULU. Get up.

GESCHWITZ. Trample me to death.

LULU. Get up or I'll scream.

GESCHWITZ. Trample me. Trample me.

LULU. Get up!

GESCHWITZ. Trample me into oblivion.

LULU. I wouldn't touch you with my foot.

GESCHWITZ. Trample me!

LULU. I'll open the door!

GESCHWITZ. Trample me. Crush me.

LULU. Go to the Moulin Rouge. You'll find somebody there.

GESCHWITZ. My love . . . my life . . .

LULU. Buy yourself a girl! Buy Bianetta!

GESCHWITZ. Just one night.

LULU. No, never! Not for a million marks!

> GESCHWITZ *rises to her feet.*

GESCHWITZ. Wretch that I am.

> *The double doors fly open and in come* BIANETTA,
> LUDMILA, MADELEINE, KADEGA, RODRIGO,
> CASTI-PIANI, PUNTSCHU, ALWA *and* BOB.

ALWA. We're going to the buffet. Tu viens, ma chérie?

MADELEINE. Everybody's won.

BIANETTA. The bank won too.

LUDMILA. That's absurd . . . C'est impossible . . . !

MADELEINE. C'est merveilleux!

ALWA. Banknotes seem to sort of unpack themselves from nothing.

PUNTSCHU. Follow me, ladies!

> *They exit in the direction of the buffet.* GESCHWITZ, *very
> upset, goes out towards the buffet.* RODRIGO *lingers.*

LULU. What do you want?

RODRIGO. I need a favour.

LULU. How much is it this time?

RODRIGO. Fifty thousand francs.

LULU *laughs*.

LULU. I haven't got it.

RODRIGO. But your husband's got it. He won't cut you off.

LULU. If anyone cuts me off, it won't be him.

RODRIGO. Then ask him.

LULU. Ask him yourself!

RODRIGO. He'll spit in my face. But he'd give it to you. He'll give you anything you want. You'll just have to sleep with him, that's all.

LULU. I can't.

RODRIGO. Why not?

LULU. Because I'm revolted by him.

RODRIGO. He *is* your husband.

LULU. I don't care.

RODRIGO. He loves you. He'd give you his whole damn fortune for just one night of love.

LULU. One night of daylight robbery.

RODRIGO. Do it, or I'll call the police.

LULU. You too?

She laughs.

Oh, turn me in! Just do it. What does it matter? I haven't got fifty thousand francs.

RODRIGO. But I want to get married.

LULU. To Bianetta?

RODRIGO. God forbid! No, this is serious. Remember my act at the Folies Bergère? That one-night wonder? Well, my consolation was that in the course of my quick-change I met one Celestine Rabeux on the wardrobe-staff. She loves me for myself, you see. To her, a man's worth more than the size of his dumb-bells. And she'll marry me too, as long as I match her savings. Fifty thousand. That's my aim. This life of debauchery's all very well for people like you, you see. But I'm the stable type. I want a wife. A couple of in-laws. Regular hours. And a line of kids to march to the church on a Sunday morning.

LULU. And for that, you would turn me in?

RODRIGO. I would if I had to.

LULU. You're so depressing.

RODRIGO. Everyone tells me that. That's why my comedy act was such a failure.

LULU. Fifty thousand francs is a lot to ask.

RODRIGO. Be nice to your husband. Nobody's saying you've got to enjoy it.

LULU. You're such a thug that it's almost sweet.

RODRIGO. You see? You do still love me a little.

He offers her his arm. In his terrible French:

Permettez-moi, Madame?

LULU. Save me a place.

RODRIGO *goes out towards the gaming-room.* LULU *stays where she is. Gets out her shares. Counts.*

Five thousand . . . eight . . .

BOB *comes on from one door, carrying a telegram on a tray.* KADEGA *comes on from another door.* LULU *watches. The two children don't see her. It's as though she's remembering a scene from her childhood.*

KADEGA. Have you seen my mother?

BOB. No.

KADEGA. I've been looking for ages.

BOB. She's probably gone up there.

He points.

KADEGA. Up where?

BOB. To the second floor.

KADEGA. What has she gone up there for?

BOB. It's nice. I'll show you. We can hide under the stairs.

KADEGA. Why would we want to do that?

BOB. Come on. You'll see.

KADEGA. I can't. I'll get into trouble.

BOB. I'll show you something.

KADEGA. What?

BOB. You'll find out.

KADEGA. What is it?

BOB. Something interesting.

KADEGA. What's interesting about it?

BOB. You'll know if you see it.

KADEGA. Tell me about it.

BOB. That's no good.

KADEGA. Then I'll look at it here.

BOB. No, it has to be there. Come on!

KADEGA. I don't want to.

BOB. Oh well . . . ! Too bad.

He makes as though to go.

KADEGA. Is it dark up there?

BOB. Why don't you see for yourself?

He gestures to the exit.

KADEGA. Well . . . just for a minute.

BOB. After you!

MADELEINE *enters from the buffet.* BOB *looks as innocent as he can.*

MADELEINE. There you are!

She slaps KADEGA*'s face.*

Never escape my sight, do you hear me?

KADEGA. I couldn't find you, Maman.

MADELEINE. Did I ask you to look?

She hugs her.

Don't cry, don't cry.

PUNTSCHU, ALWA, BIANETTA, LUDMILA, GESCHWITZ *and* CASTI-PIANI *appear from the buffet en route back to the gaming-room. Of* KADEGA*:*

LUDMILA. Poor little thing!

CASTI-PIANI. How pretty she is, with tears in her eyes!

PUNTSCHU. The unshorn lamb.

CASTI-PIANI. The unplucked rose.

BOB *raises his tray and calls:*

BOB. Telegram for Monsieur Puntschu.

PUNTSCHU. I'm here!

ALWA. And back to the game!

BOB *gives* PUNTSCHU *the telegram and he reads it.* BOB *goes out. The others start going into the gaming-room.* CASTI-PIANI *stops by* LULU.

CASTI-PIANI. What were you talking about?

LULU. Who with?

CASTI-PIANI. That jumping bean.

LULU. Oh . . . lovers' talk.

CASTI-PIANI. I'll give you twenty-four hours to come up with the money.

He turns to PUNTSCHU.

Herr Puntschu, I shall clean you out.

PUNTSCHU *has finished reading his telegram. To*
CASTIPIANI:

PUNTSCHU. The life of finance! My smile holds no
attractions. Nobody wants my private organs. So I use my
brain instead. It serves me well. It doesn't sag and wrinkle,
it won't catch pox and it doesn't need to be washed each
time I've used it.

He puts his arm around CASTI-PIANI's *shoulder and they
go into the gaming room.* BOB *shows in* SCHIGOLCH.

BOB. You have a visitor, Madame.

LULU. Show him in.

SCHIGOLCH *comes in. He glances at* BOB *as he leaves.*

SCHIGOLCH. Who's that?

LULU. My under footman.

SCHIGOLCH. What does he do?

LULU. I'm training him up.

SCHIGOLCH. Promising is he?

LULU. He's learning fast. What do you want this time?

SCHIGOLCH. Five hundred francs. I've got to furnish my
little attic. It isn't fit for *me*, let alone my mistress.

LULU. You've got a mistress?

SCHIGOLCH. Yes, with God's good help.

LULU. But you're ancient!

SCHIGOLCH. What do you think I came to Paris for?

He laughs. LULU *is shaking with fear and distress.*

What's wrong, my sweetie?

LULU. I can't take any more. It's all too . . .

SCHIGOLCH. What?

LULU. Too frightening.

She puts her head on his lap and cries convulsively.

Help me.

SCHIGOLCH. Scream, my darling. Scream out loud. Wash in snow. Take salt baths. Spend one day a week in bed with a novel.

He strokes her in fatherly manner.

I had you on my knee, when was it . . . ? Twenty years ago. It seems like yesterday. You'd cry like now. I'd stroke your hair, like this, and rub your knees. You had no white satin gown in those days . . . nor no feathers in your hair, nor stockings. Hardly a shirt. Don't cry, don't cry.

LULU. I've been betrayed. They're going to hand me over to the police.

SCHIGOLCH. Who is? Give me a name.

LULU. Rodrigo.

SCHIGOLCH. Him? I'll talk him out of it. I'll buy him a drink.

LULU. I want you to kill him.

SCHIGOLCH. He isn't worth the trouble.

LULU. Kill him!

SCHIGOLCH. He's just an idiot.

LULU. For the sake of your daughter!

SCHIGOLCH. Don't be too sure. You could be anyone's daughter.

LULU. Promise you'll kill him.

SCHIGOLCH. I could drop him in the Seine, I suppose. But what do I get?

LULU. Five hundred francs.

SCHIGOLCH. I didn't hear you.

LULU. A thousand.

SCHIGOLCH. Put it like this. If I took up killing people for money, I'd be rich.

LULU. What do you want? Don't ask too much.

SCHIGOLCH. Well, now . . . if ever you felt nostalgic . . . for our old arrangement . . .

LULU. Oh God . . . !

SCHIGOLCH. Why not?

LULU. I'm . . . changed. I'm not a child any more.

SCHIGOLCH. What do you see when you look at me now? Some aged monster?

LULU. But you've already got a mistress.

SCHIGOLCH. She's sixty-five.

LULU. What do you do with her?

SCHIGOLCH. We play cards of an evening.

LULU. What would you want from me?

SCHIGOLCH. Have you forgotten? Never you mind. It'll all come back.

LULU *gets up*.

LULU. All right. I'll do it. But you must do . . . what I've just asked you.

SCHIGOLCH. And you'll come to my attic?

LULU. Whenever you like.

SCHIGOLCH. Soixante quinze Quai de la Gare.

LULU. I've got that.

SCHIGOLCH. Wear white satin.

LULU. You'll tear it off me.

SCHIGOLCH. Pearls and diamonds.

LULU. I'll come as I am.

SCHIGOLCH. My funeral banquet.

LULU. But you must swear you'll kill him.

SCHIGOLCH. Send him round.

LULU. Swear it!

He gropes beneath her skirt.

Swear! By all that's sacred.

SCHIGOLCH. By all that's sacred.

LULU. How cold that feels!

SCHIGOLCH. You're burning with hatred, girl.

Pause, as LULU *moves away, rearranges her dress, settles her hair in the mirror and dries her eyes.*

LULU. Go home. I want you there when they arrive.

SCHIGOLCH. They?

LULU. I'll get the Countess to bring him. Tell him the room is hers. And that you live next-door. Get them drunk. Wait until she's passed out. Then . . .

SCHIGOLCH. I'll use my knife. Then out he goes into the river. It's three steps up to the window, mind. I'll have to roll him.

LULU. Bring me his earring. Oh . . . !

SCHIGOLCH. What's the matter?

LULU. My garter's snapped.

She lifts her dress and re-ties her garter.

SCHIGOLCH. What a scent!

LULU. Remember the earring. Go.

She opens the door for him. He goes. RODRIGO *comes in from the gaming-room.*

RODRIGO. I thought you were going to play.

LULU. It's been a busy evening. I've arranged that fifty thousand. But there's something you must do for me in return.

RODRIGO. What's that?

LULU. Get the Countess off my hands. Make love to her.

RODRIGO. Not that!

LULU. Have you never had an aristocrat before?

RODRIGO. Oh, dozens. Duchesses, princesses . . . Only they'd got thighs and breasts and bums . . .

LULU. She's got thighs of a sort.

RODRIGO. I couldn't do it. Haven't the strength.

LULU. You're supposed to be a strong-man.

RODRIGO. That's just my biceps.

LULU. But she's desperate for you!

RODRIGO. I can't believe it!

LULU. Oh but it's true. You can thank your rippling tummy-muscles.

RODRIGO. Well . . . if I must. But it's fifty thousand.

He starts off for the buffet.

LULU. Where are you going?

RODRIGO. I need a drink. What awesome challenge can a man not rise to?

He's gone. LULU *opens the door of the gaming-room and calls:*

LULU. Countess . . .

GESCHWITZ *comes in.*

GESCHWITZ. Lulu . . . ?

LULU. If you do as I say tonight . . . are you listening to me . . . ?

GESCHWITZ. If I do as you say tonight . . . Then what?

LULU. Tomorrow night I'll let you . . .

GESCHWITZ. Let me what?

LULU. Sleep with me.

GESCHWITZ *grabs* LULU*'s hand and covers it with kisses.*

GESCHWITZ. Thank you!

LULU. You can undress me . . .

GESCHWITZ. Oh . . .

LULU. Undo my hair . . .

GESCHWITZ. Oh, Lulu . . .

LULU . . . . untie my stockings . . .

She takes away her hand.

But first . . .

GESCHWITZ. First what? Just tell me.

LULU. I want you to go with Rodrigo.

GESCHWITZ. What for?

LULU. Surely you know what for.

GESCHWITZ. Do you mean . . . make love? Make love with a man?

LULU. Yes. Aren't you excited?

GESCHWITZ. Lulu . . . ask me anything . . . anything else . . . however appalling.

LULU. It's not so bad. I didn't want it either, my first time. And I was young then. I could hardly count to three. But I got over it.

GESCHWITZ. Take my life. Take all I have left. Don't make me do this!

LULU. Perhaps he'll cure you.

GESCHWITZ. Cure me of love? It isn't a sickness.

She turns away, cries.

LULU. Do you think I would offer you . . . myself . . . if there weren't someone threatening to betray me? To sell me to . . . Or worse than that. To send me home to be beheaded? You're my only escape.

GESCHWITZ. Tell me what to do.

LULU. Ask him. Plead.

GESCHWITZ. For what?

LULU. Oh, don't pretend!

GESCHWITZ. I'm not pretending. I really don't know. I've never done this before.

LULU. Tell him you love him. Men get angry if you don't.

GESCHWITZ. I'll try.

LULU. Then take a cab, and say to the driver . . . 'Soixante quinze Quai de la Gare'.

GESCHWITZ. Yes.

LULU. 'Soixante quinze Quai de la Gare.'

GESCHWITZ. Yes.

LULU. Shall I write it down?

GESCHWITZ. Yes.

  LULU *writes it down on a card.*

LULU. You'll have to pay the driver.

  She gives GESCHWITZ *the card.*

GESCHWITZ (*taking it*). Yes.

LULU. Go up to the attic. It belongs to a friend. You must say that it's yours.

  She opens the door. Calls:

Monsieur, s'il vous plaît.

  RODRIGO *comes in, still eating.* LULU, *moving past* GESCHWITZ, *whispers:*

LULU. Don't be shy.

  Looking at the floor, GESCHWITZ *walks towards* RODRIGO *and throws her arms around his neck.*

RODRIGO. That's a start.

LULU. Take a cab. There's a rank outside.

RODRIGO *groans under* GESCHWITZ*'s embrace.*

RODRIGO. Let go, you're squeezing.

GESCHWITZ *stares into his eyes.*

GESCHWITZ. I love you.

She tries to drag him along with her.

RODRIGO. Jesus!

GESCHWITZ. Please.

RODRIGO. Who would have thought the old nag had it in her?

GESCHWITZ *recoils, puts her hands over her face.*

GESCHWITZ. This is impossible!

LULU. Do it!

GESCHWITZ. He's so crude!

RODRIGO. What kind of brute do you think I am? If you don't want *me*, I'll bring you a thingamajig tomorrow that only needs winding-up to give you the time of your life. Just don't try it on me, that's all!

GESCHWITZ. God, oh God!

LULU (*quietly to* RODERIGO). Fifty thousand.

GESCHWITZ. Lulu, I can't!

LULU (*quietly to* GESCHWITZ). It's life and death.

GESCHWITZ *steels herself. To* RODRIGO*:*

GESCHWITZ. Come on, come on . . . I want you . . . I want whatever you've got to give . . . all over me.

RODRIGO (*reassured*). That's more like it . . . dirty old cow . . . come on, let's mount the scaffold.

He leads her out. GESCHWITZ *says quickly and quietly, as she passes* LULU*:*

GESCHWITZ. This will kill me.

They have gone.

LULU. I'm so tired.

She checks the value of her shares.

LULU. Fourteen thousand . . . fifteen . . . I can do it.

A monstrous noise is heard from the gaming-room.
PUNTSCHU *emerges, followed by* CASTI-PIANI, ALWA,
BIANETTA, MADELEINE, KADEGA *and* LUDMILA.
ALWA *is holding up a bunch of share certificates.*

ALWA. You *must* accept! You have to!

PUNTSCHU. Certainly not! Pay me in cash!

LULU. What's the matter?

LUDMILA. Something strange is happening with our shares.

ALWA (*points at* PUNTSCHU). He sold them to us!

MADELEINE (*annoyed, to* ALWA). Why are you causing this
disturbance?

PUNTSCHU. Those share certificates are not legal tender.

ALWA. Look! He's quitting the game!

PUNTSCHU. I'm quitting while I'm ahead! What's wrong
with that?

LUDMILA. These double-dealing Prussians.

MADELEINE. What's happening?

PUNTSCHU. Devil take it! I shall be in my office at ten
o'clock tomorrow. Let him come to me then, with genuine
money.

ALWA *brandishes his share certificates.*

ALWA. Look here, you swine, you swindler . . .

MADELEINE. What is he saying about our shares?

PUNTSCHU. Let's all be reasonable, my friend. Those shares
are mere waste paper.

LUDMILA. What?

BIANETTA. What?

LULU. What?

MADELEINE. What's going on?

ALWA (*to* PUNTSCHU). You were the man who *sold* us these! What do you say to that?

PUNTSCHU. What I can say, dear fellow, is that according to this telegram, which I have just received, . . .

He produces it.

. . . shares in the Jungfrau funicular railway, after their peak of three hundred and forty, have now sunk to a mere fifteen and show no sign of stopping.

MADELEINE. Mon Dieu!!

She faints. KADEGA *throws herself upon her.*

KADEGA. Maman!

CASTI-PIANI *leaves quickly.*

ALWA (*to* PUNTSCHU). Why didn't you tell us?

PUNTSCHU. I was reluctant to disseminate confusion.

ALWA. We're ruined!

LULU. We're out on the streets.

PUNTSCHU (*lying*). What about me? I've lost a fortune.

KADEGA *is bent over her mother.*

KADEGA. Maman is dying!

PUNTSCHU. Let's hope she stays that way. She'll kill me if she ever comes round.

He starts to go.

BIANETTA (*to* PUNTSCHU). Where are you going, Monsieur?

PUNTSCHU. Why, in Paris one is spoiled for opportunity.

BIANETTA. Will you offer me dinner at Silvain's?

PUNTSCHU. My dear Bianetta . . . ! Why do you wish for dinner with *me*?

BIANETTA. I'm sorry for you, Monsieur. You've lost a fortune.

PUNTSCHU. Nothing is quite as simple as that . . . where there are losers, there are winners . . . it's a complicated matter . . . I'll explain it to you . . .

He and BIANETTA *go. All have now gone except for* LULU, ALWA, KADEGA *and* MADELEINE, *who is still unconscious.*

LULU. Where's Casti-Piani?

ALWA. Who cares?

LULU. He's gone to the police.

ALWA. Stop panicking.

LULU. We've been betrayed. You'll go to prison and I'll have my head cut off.

ALWA. To prison!

LULU. Get the safe. Hide it under your coat. Meet me outside at the kitchen entrance.

ALWA. Betrayed by who?

LULU. Oh, what does it matter?

ALWA. By Casti-Piani? How did he know? Is he your lover?

LULU. What do you think? Just go!

They go. MADELEINE *comes round.*

MADELEINE. Where am I?

KADEGA. Everyone's run away, Maman. Can we go home now?

MADELEINE *sits up.*

MADELEINE. We're destitute.

KADEGA. I don't mind. I didn't want to go back to the convent anyway. I'll work!

MADELEINE. You're only thirteen!

KADEGA. That doesn't matter.

MADELEINE. *I* could work. I might try for an engagement at the Opéra Comique. My voice is still pretty enough . . .

KADEGA. Take me with you.

MADELEINE. Certainly not! To a place like that! To the Olympia, perhaps . . . Yes, that might do . . . You'll need a patron . . . you must lower your expectations, darling . . .

KADEGA. I'll do whatever you want.

MADELEINE. You might regret it.

KADEGA. Not in a million years. I'd die for you, Maman. If only it meant that somebody gave you lots of money.

MADELEINE. There's the Baron Fouquet. Though he's sixty-five . . . you wouldn't object to a man like him, my darling? Would you?

The CHIEF OF POLICE *and as many gendarmes as possible burst into the room.*

CHIEF OF POLICE. Stop in the name of the law! You're charged with murder!

KADEGA. Help! Help!

Two of the gendarmes grab KADEGA *and carry her screaming off-stage. Others put* MADELEINE *in handcuffs. She screams too.* CASTI-PIANI *appears and sees what's happening:*

CASTI-PIANI. Not *that* one!

End of Act Four.

ACT FIVE

London. An attic room. An old green chaise-longue. A torn grey mattress on the floor. A flowerstand, painted red: on it, a bottle of whisky and a smoking oil-lamp. The walls of the attic have been washed over with red paint.

Rain is beating down on the roof. Water drips through the skylight. The floorboards are flooded.

SCHIGOLCH *lies on the mattress.He wears a long grey greatcoat, reaching down to his feet.* ALWA *lies on the chaiselongue, wrapped in a red tartan rug. The strap belonging to the rug hangs above him on the wall.*

LULU, *her hair now half-length, comes in carrying a washing-bowl.*

SCHIGOLCH. Where'd you get to, girl?

ALWA. She had to wash herself.

SCHIGOLCH. What for? The English girls don't bother.

ALWA. This one's got style.

    LULU *puts the basin under the wash-stand. To her:*

    You can't wait to see me buried, can you?

LULU. No I can't. I wish you were both dead.

    ALWA *rolls over on to his back.*

ALWA. Listen to her . . . my wife . . . my wife!

LULU. You're not worth the knock on the head it would take to shut you up.

SCHIGOLCH (*to* ALWA). They always grizzle and whine to start with. It's like any other job. She's got to work her way into it. This time next week there'll be no stopping her.

LULU *sits on the floor, her back against the wall, and throws her arms around her knees.*

LULU. I'm cold.

ALWA. I dreamt we were dining at Sylvain's.

SCHIGOLCH (*mutters to himself*). She's got the languages.

ALWA. Bianetta was with us. I ordered *fers de cheval*. I couldn't get them out of their shells. But I could feel them in my stomach. I was crying with happiness. I was so drunk, that the glass kept missing my mouth. Champagne was running down the front of my shirt.

SCHIGOLCH. Yes, yes.

LULU. I can't even feel my hands. My feet have gone dead.

SCHIGOLCH. She's wasting time. She'll miss the theatre crowd.

LULU. I'd rather stay here and freeze to death.

ALWA. She's right. We're dying anyway. Why prolong the misery?

LULU. You'll take the money though, won't you? I've got to squeeze out the last bit of life I've got and stuff it in your mouth for food.

ALWA. Not mine. I won't accept it.

SCHIGOLCH. What's she moaning about? She's been doing it since she was a kiddie.

LULU. You're drunk.

SCHIGOLCH. She was a breadwinner at ten years old.

ALWA *writhes*.

ALWA. I'm starving! Get me a beefsteak, Katya! My kingdom for a . . .

SCHIGOLCH. Kick her down the stairs. I haven't the strength. I'm just a frail old man.

LULU. Once I've walked the street, I'll never get off it. That's what it's like. You get that 'look', you can't go anywhere else. It's too late now. My clothes are in rags. You've worn me out.

ALWA. I dreamt of a cigarette. It was the whitest, fattest, juiciest cigarette that had ever been rolled. It was the smoke of smokes.

LULU. There are men out there, you can't even see the faces of. With their hats pulled down and their collars turned up, and their hands pushed into their pockets. Why should I go with people like that? I don't owe you anything. I've never cost you a penny. He's a writer. Why isn't he working? Why doesn't *he* make money?

ALWA. Who degraded me? Who killed my hopes? Who ruined my inspiration?

LULU. You fool. You clown.

ALWA. Who made me kill my father?

LULU. Who shot him? Not you, you idle bastard. I'd like to chop off my hands for what I did. He didn't lose much by dying, it's true. He didn't have much to lose. But compared to you . . .

ALWA. What you see is what you've made of me.

LULU. You came begging to me. You crawled.

ALWA. I was a bright young hope. And I threw it away. I whored it away. Oh, God forgive me!

SCHIGOLCH (*to* LULU). You're making him ill.

ALWA. I squandered my money on women. On men. I might as well have stuffed it down the gutter.

SCHIGOLCH. You were unlucky, old son.

LULU. He was a mug.

SCHIGOLCH. Hear what she said? That's women for you. I don't understand them.

ALWA. I never have.

LULU. I do.

ALWA. At least in Paris you know what they're thinking. Not
like here. One fine lady wanted *me* to pay *her*. She broke
my walking-stick. I shouted 'Police!' and she picked up a
pile of horse-shit and threw it at me. That's your English
fille de joie! At least I'm stuck in bed now. No more prowling.
Never again. But the more I starve, the more I want it!
Katya! If I'm forced to choose between you and going mad
with frustration . . . Here! Come here!

*He gets up, his trousers around his ankles, and hobbles
towards* LULU.

LULU. Go to the hospital! You're sick!

ALWA. Who made me sick?

LULU. Not me!

SCHIGOLCH. Oh, she'll give pleasure to thousands yet.

LULU. Get away!

She pushes ALWA *away, forcing him down on to the floor.*

ALWA. Vampire. Bitch. I'll kill you. Then I'll suck your veins.

LULU. I've kept my innocence all my life. Only to drown in
filth.

She sits at the end of SCHIGOLCH'*s mattress and rests her
elbows on her knees.*

SCHIGOLCH. Get out. Go on. We're hungry.

LULU. Let me put my feet inside your coat.

SCHIGOLCH. If only you had those knickers of Chinese silk
that you used to wear . . . that and the garters . . .

LULU. Just for a moment.

SCHIGOLCH. Go on then.

She puts her feet inside his coat.

LULU. Button it up. I'm cold.

SCHIGOLCH. Ever since Paris, I've lacked all feeling in my
fingers. They're getting blue. I'll go out for a drink in a bit.

Round midnight. Pub on the corner. There's a nice little
English blonde behind the bar . . .

LULU. Oh, for God's sake.

She gets up. Takes a swig of whisky.

SCHIGOLCH (*to* ALWA). That's nice, that's lovely. Now they
can smell the drink at twenty paces.

LULU. I've left you plenty.

She prepares to go out. Sits to lace up her boots.

How I dread those stairs.

Stops.

I can feel the . . .

Stops, stands.

Feel the . . .

Stands.

Ah je jouirai . . . Ah je jouirai . . .

*She shivers from the cold. There's a knock at the door. It
opens. The* COUNTESS GESCHWITZ *is there, pale and
shabbily-dressed. She carries a rolled-up canvas.*

GESCHWITZ. Forgive me . . . If I've come at an inconvenient
time . . .

LULU. It's late.

GESCHWITZ. I haven't spoken to anyone else for the last ten
days.

LULU. Did you bring any money?

GESCHWITZ. No. I wrote to my brother. He hasn't replied.
I've nothing left. I've not eaten today. Lulu . . .

LULU. I'm going out.

GESCHWITZ. Lulu!

SCHIGOLCH (*of the canvas*). What's that?

GESCHWITZ (*to* LULU). I've brought you something.

LULU (*not listening*). I must be mad.

GESCHWITZ. It's her portrait.

ALWA. Is it? Let me see it.

LULU. I ought to drown myself.

ALWA *takes the canvas and unrolls it. It's the Pierrot portrait, now cracked and stained.*

ALWA. It's her! We've got her back!

LULU. What's that?

GESCHWITZ. It's you.

LULU *sees it. She's horrified.*

LULU. Oh God! Not that!

SCHIGOLCH. We ought to stick it up on the wall.

GESCHWITZ. I went back to the house in Paris the day you left. I cut it out of its frame. The paint has cracked a little. I was as careful with it as I could be.

ALWA (*at the wall*). Here's a nail.

SCHIGOLCH. It needs another at the bottom.

ALWA. I'll do it.

He takes a nail out of the wall, takes off his boot and hammers the nail through the canvas.

SCHIGOLCH. Note of luxury. Raises the tone.

GESCHWITZ. A man in Drury Lane offered me half a crown for it. I wouldn't sell it to him.

ALWA. It'll hang out flat. (*To* LULU.) Bring the lamp.

She does. They look at the portrait.

She had everything a man could need.

LULU *laughs.*

SCHIGOLCH. They can look at that . . . and fill in the gaps for themselves.

LULU *laughs*.

ALWA. She's thinner now.

SCHIGOLCH. Who isn't?

ALWA. But the eyes are the same.

SCHIGOLCH. As for the rest . . . at least she can say, that's what she *was*.

LULU *laughs*.

ALWA. She was exactly this. The look . . . the mouth . . . the skin . . .

GESCHWITZ. The painter must have been immensely gifted.

LULU *laughs*.

ALWA. Didn't you know him?

GESCHWITZ. He was before my time.

SCHIGOLCH. You don't see legs like that any more.

ALWA (*of the painted image*). Every thought which crosses her mind is joyful. Her inner desires are wakening to the dawn. Her lips are thoughts of kisses.

SCHIGOLCH. She is a grace bestowed by heaven.

ALWA. Now at last I see the tragedy of my life.

SCHIGOLCH. I knew that mouth when it would suck my finger.

ALWA. It's Nature's cruellest trick. Women's beauty blossoms for a moment . . . but it enslaves us for a lifetime . . .

SCHIGOLCH. She'll still pass muster at the foot of a lamp-post.

ALWA . . . . and where's the disgrace in being enslaved by Nature?

LULU *puts the lamp back on the flower-stand*.

LULU. I won't be long.

GESCHWITZ. Where are you going?

ALWA. She's going to prostitute herself.

GESCHWITZ. Lulu!

There are tears in LULU*'s eyes.*

LULU. Don't make it worse for me.

GESCHWITZ. I'll come with you.

LULU. Leave me alone, you cripple.

LULU *goes out.*

GESCHWITZ. I'll go instead. I'll take her place.

SCHIGOLCH. Stay off her beat! You'll frighten the customers.

GESCHWITZ *goes after* LULU.

Damn. Damn. That's all we need. Why didn't you grab her?

ALWA *is looking at the picture.*

ALWA. Looking at that . . . remembering how she was . . .

SCHIGOLCH. She'll bury us all. Let's not get maudlin.

ALWA. The day we met, I was fifteen. She was sitting in a rocking-chair, with just her blouse on. And a pair of Turkish slippers. We felt like brother and sister. We talked about a poem of mine. It was the first I'd written. 'Set loose your hounds towards the furthest hills . . . they will return transformed by sweat and dust . . . '

SCHIGOLCH. Yes, yes, yes.

ALWA. Then later . . . we danced together at the New Year's Ball. She wore pink tulle, with a white bodice. Dr. Goll had brought her . . . they weren't yet married. Papa had to pretend he didn't know her. So we danced together all night. Papa never took his eyes off us. Mamma arrived, conspicuously late. She'd had a headache.

SCHIGOLCH (*mutters*). How'll she manage . . . with that old freak running after her . . . ?

ALWA. The first time we made love, she was in her wedding-dress. All soft and rustly. As though she was wrapped in tissue-paper. But the bridegroom was my father. She'd mixed us up.

Footsteps can be heard on the stairs.

SCHIGOLCH. Here she is.

He indicates a small cubby-hole.

We'll hide in there.

ALWA. What if he takes advantage of her?

SCHIGOLCH. What if he doesn't?

ALWA. I'll kill him if he . . .

SCHIGOLCH. Be quiet! Get in!

They get in. LULU *comes in with* MR. HOPKINS.

LULU. This is my room.

HOPKINS *is an enormous man with a clean-shaven, pink face. Blue eyes and a friendly smile. He wears a top hat and a long havelock cape and carries a dripping umbrella in one hand. He lays a finger over his mouth and looks at* LULU *with an air of significance.*

It's not very comfortable.

HOPKINS *puts his hand over her mouth and lays an index-finger on his lips. She frees herself.*

There's nobody here. Don't worry.

He puts his finger to his lips again. He takes off his cape, folds it up and puts it down neatly, opens his umbrella and stands it to dry.

SCHIGOLCH (*behind the door*). Where did she pick up this one?

ALWA. I swear I'll murder him.

SCHIGOLCH. Ssh!

HOPKINS grins, takes hold of LULU *with both hands and kisses her forehead.* LULU *steps back.*

LULU. Have you got any money?

Gently, HOPKINS *holds her mouth closed and presses a ten-shilling piece into her hand.* LULU *looks at it, passing it from one hand to the other. He looks at her questioningly. She puts it into her pocket.*

All right.

He quickly gives her another five shillings. Stares at her in masterful fashion.

That's very generous.

HOPKINS *jumps around the room as though mad, punches the air and stares desperately upwards.* LULU *approaches him, throws her arms around his waist, lays her index finger on his lips and shakes her head. He takes her head in both hands and kisses her on the mouth. She puts her arms around him and kisses him on the lips.*

HOPKINS *frees himself, laughs silently and glances with meaning first at the mattress and then at the chaise-longue.* LULU *takes the lamp, looks meaningfully at* HOPKINS *and opens the door to the bedroom. Smiles and goes in.* HOPKINS *nods and steps in, raising his hat. Now the room is dark except for a ray of light from under the bedroom door.*

ALWA *is on all fours.*

ALWA. They've gone into the bedroom.

SCHIGOLCH. Ssh! Get back!

ALWA. They can't hear us.

LULU *comes out of the bedroom. She collects the basin from under the wash-stand. Seeing* ALWA *and* SCHIGOLCH, *she frowns and gestures to them to stay hidden away. She goes back into the bedroom with the basin.*

Now.

SCHIGOLCH *picks up* HOPKINS*'s cape and rifles through the pockets.* ALWA, *meanwhile, has crept to the door of the bedroom.*

SCHIGOLCH. Gloves . . .

He searches the inside pocket. Takes out a small book. Reads:

'Lessons for Christian Workers . . . with a preface by the Reverend W. Hay. Three shillings and sixpence.' Truly this is a nation in decline.

The door to the bedroom opens and Mr. HOPKINS *comes out, half-dressed. Seeing* SCHIGOLCH *rifling the cape, he rushes at him with an expression of rage, passing* ALWA *en route.* ALWA *leaps on to him from behind.* LULU *comes out from the bedroom with the lamp. She screams.*

LULU. Leave him alone!

HOPKINS *shakes off* ALWA *with ease, deals him a mighty blow, grabs his cape and dashes out of the main door and down the stairs, leaving* ALWA *on the floor.* LULU *pulls herself up. Stands shaking.*

LULU. I'm going back out. It isn't so hard. I ask the time. Then I say, 'What are you doing out so late?' Or, 'Why do you look so sad?' You've got to look as though you'll understand them.

She glances at ALWA.

Alwa?

SCHIGOLCH. Out for the count. He's only himself to blame.

LULU *goes.* SCHIGOLCH *looks at* ALWA. *Feels his head.*

Blood? More blood.

He gets the lamp. Shouts in ALWA*'s ear:*

Alwa! (*To himself.*) He's gone deaf.

He puts his fingers on ALWA*'s temples.*

No fever.

He opens one of ALWA*'s eyes with his thumb.*

Better put him to bed.

He puts one arm under ALWA*'s shoulders and another under his knees. Tries to lift him but drops him.*

Why'd I do that? He doesn't weigh much. (*To* ALWA.) Wakey wakey! Lazy good-for-nothing. You've got the whole world before you.

He shakes him.

Don't sulk. He didn't intend to be so hard on you. You caught him off-guard, that's all. You can still . . . Whatever you want. Whenever you like.

He sits up.

Take your time. Don't mind me. I'll wait. You've got a nice long while to make your mind up. Give us a smile . . . ? I thought so . . . Lump of sugar?

He half-lifts ALWA, *as before, and drags him a few paces. Puts him down.*

Either . . . or. That's the choice. It's one or the other. No middle way. You hear me?

Shouts.

Hear me!?

He boxes ALWA *about the ears.*

You think about that.

He looks round. Gazes at LULU*'s portrait.*

What is it about a picture? Nobody ever hangs them straight. There's something . . . snow-white legs . . . arm in the air . . . whoever held their arm in the air like that? Like in a dream. Like death. Closer and closer every day. But when you're old . . . and so many things have shot up into the air . . . and faded . . . you don't go fainting in dismay . . . you don't go cutting your throat . . . you buy a whisky and a portion of pie.

He looks at ALWA.

It's bed-time.

He drags ALWA *out of sight. The door to the stairs opens.* GESCHWITZ *comes in, not making a sound. She stands still.* SCHIGOLCH *comes back.*

SCHIGOLCH. Is it you?

GESCHWITZ. It's me.

SCHIGOLCH. I thought you were . . . the next one.

Pause.

GESCHWITZ. He's coming up.

SCHIGOLCH. Better not disturb him.

GESCHWITZ. Don't let me keep you.

SCHIGOLCH. I'll stay out of his way.

Pause.

GESCHWITZ. It's dark.

SCHIGOLCH. It'll get darker.

GESCHWITZ. She says I'm crippled.

SCHIGOLCH. We all of us have our faults.

GESCHWITZ. I can't be with her. And I can't be without her.

SCHIGOLCH. Maybe, because you're flat in the front, you'll never be happy till you're in charge.

GESCHWITZ. I've learned to be patient.

SCHIGOLCH. That's good. Because you'll never compete with her in the chest department.

GESCHWITZ *moves away.*

GESCHWITZ. She told me to wait.

SCHIGOLCH. I'll probably pass her on the stairs.

He goes.

GESCHWITZ. 'Crippled'. She's right. I've waited for her for three whole years. I was her murder-weapon. She lied. She lied. Three years for a single minute. The only thing I haven't given her is the sight of myself lying dead on the ground before her. That's all I have to offer. Everything else has gone. My money, my share of my father's estate, my joy, my dignity. And still I wait. But what would I gain from dying? I doubt she'd notice. I don't even believe in God any more. That God who crippled me. Who made me crippled.

She opens her bag. Takes out a revolver. Lays it on her lap.

If he comes down now, I'll shoot him. Him and his kind. They're not crippled. They're whole. They're sturdy. Every ragged, common beggar off the street. She'll bless each one of them. Why not me? Why am I cursed like this?

She raises the gun to her head. Puts it down.

Better to hang. No noise. What have I got to look forward to? Pain. More pain. I could jump off a bridge. The water is cold. My bed is cold. Which of the two is colder? If only the stairwells weren't so paltry. They were taller in Paris. I cannot believe the water is cold for long. I would dream of her till the end. No, hanging is best. Or stab myself with a knife. But stabbing to *death?* It wouldn't work. I haven't the blood in me. It wouldn't come out. How I've dreamt of her kisses. One more . . . then another . . . but it's always interrupted. I can't cut my veins . . . I can't take poison . . . I cannot defile the Thames with *what I am* . . .

She takes the strap from the tartan rug. Climbs on to a chair, loops the strap around her neck, fixes the end around a hook in the wall, kicks over the chair. Falls to the ground. She feels for the end of the strap and finds that it has torn the hook from the wall.

Damn this life.

She stays leaning against the wall. After a few moments:

Lulu . . . if you are testing me . . . if there is still a place to go . . . all you need do is tell me. Open your heart, however little you can. I'll wait. That's fine. That's fine. But it must

be an absolute promise. Lulu. I cannot depart my life like
this. I'd suffer forever. I'd burn for the rest of eternity. That
isn't my fate. I know it's not. I am destined to be happy.
Even if only once. It's God's good plan. There *is* a plan.
It isn't possible that pain as great as mine can have no
meaning.

She falls to the ground. On hands and feet.

Has anyone suffered like me? Has anyone given you more?
You laugh. You overflow with happiness. Look at me. My
star in heaven. My angel. Who in the world has waited
longer for you? Your skin is as soft as snow. Your heart is
colder. Pity me.

LULU *leads* JACK *in. Her eyes are sparkling. To*
GESCHWITZ:

LULU. Haven't you gone?

JACK. Who's she?

LULU. My sister. She's mad. She follows me round.

GESCHWITZ *crawls backwards like a dog.*

GESCHWITZ. I didn't hear you.

JACK. Is she a worry for us?

LULU. No. Stay. Stay. Don't go. Please.

JACK. Your mouth is beautiful when you speak.

LULU *holds opens the door. To* GESCHWITZ.

LULU. Go out. Wait on the stairs.

JACK. Don't send her away.

LULU *shuts the door.*

LULU. Will you stay with me?

JACK. How much do you charge?

LULU. For the night . . . ?

JACK. You have a strong, pretty chin. Your lips are like
bursting cherries. You aren't English?

LULU. No.

JACK. What are you?

LULU. German.

JACK. Where did you get your beautiful mouth?

LULU. From my mother.

JACK. I know that. How much do you want?

LULU. Whatever you like.

JACK. I can't waste money. I'm not Baron Rothschild.

LULU. Will you stay all night?

JACK. I haven't got time.

LULU. Why not?

JACK. I'm a married man.

LULU. You can say, you missed the last bus and you had to
    spend the night with a friend.

JACK. 'Time is money'. How much do you want?

LULU. One pound.

JACK. Good night.

He moves towards the door. She holds him back.

LULU. Wait!

JACK *goes to the cubby-hole and looks about in it.*

I'm living with my sister.

JACK. You have a fine impertinence to ask for a pound.

LULU. You can pay me in the morning.

JACK. While I'm asleep, you'll rifle my pockets.

LULU. I don't do that.

JACK. Why do you want me to stay all night?

LULU *doesn't answer.*

It's suspicious.

LULU. Just give me whatever you like.

JACK. Your mouth is the best part of you.

LULU. Ten shillings.

He laughs and goes towards the door. She holds him back.

Don't go!

JACK. How much do you want?

LULU. I don't want anything.

JACK. Why not?

GESCHWITZ *has pulled herself up, implicitly threatening* JACK. LULU *pushes her back.*

Leave her alone!

LULU *does.*

She's not your sister. She loves you.

LULU. She's my sister-in-law.

JACK *goes to* GESCHWITZ *and strokes her hair.*

JACK. We don't hurt each other. We understand each other. Don't we?

He caresses GESCHWITZ*'s cheek.*

Poor beast.

GESCHWITZ *crawls backwards, looking at* JACK.

LULU. Are you a bugger?

JACK *holds on to* GESCHWITZ *by the leather strap, which is still around her neck.*

JACK. What's this?

LULU. She is insane. I told you. If you prefer, you can go with her.

JACK *holds* GESCHWITZ *tightly. To* LULU*:*

JACK. Tell me how much you want.

LULU. Eight shillings.

JACK. That's too much.

LULU. If *that's* too much . . . !

JACK. How long have you been walking the streets?

LULU. Two years.

JACK. I don't believe that.

LULU. Since my birthday.

JACK. Why do you lie?

LULU. I started today.

JACK. Are you a mother?

LULU. I don't know what you mean.

JACK. Have you had a child?

LULU. No. Why do you ask?

JACK. Because your mouth is so fresh.

LULU. I was a nice looking woman.

JACK. How much do you want if I stay all night?

LULU. Five shillings.

JACK. No.

   He drops GESCHWITZ *and starts to go.*

   Good night.

   LULU *clings on to him.*

LULU. Give me four.

JACK. Have you a friend living with you?

LULU. I am alone. There's just her.

   JACK *points to a door.*

JACK. What's in there?

LULU. My kitchen.

JACK. Your kitchen?

LULU. There's no window in it.

He stamps on the floor.

JACK. Who lives down there?

LULU. Nobody. That room is to let.

JACK. Would three shillings be enough?

LULU. Yes.

JACK. I haven't got it.

LULU. Two?

JACK. I could tell what you were like by the way you walked.

LULU. Was I walking towards you?

JACK. No. I was following you.

LULU. My skirt is torn at the back.

JACK. I was right about you. I could see you were perfectly
    formed.

LULU. How could you tell from behind?

JACK. From the way that you put your feet. I said to myself,
    she has an expressive mouth.

LULU. You liked my mouth?

JACK. I did. You're clever. You're ambitious. You're good-
    hearted.

LULU. What's wrong with that?

JACK. Nothing. It's what I saw from how you walked on the
    pavement.

LULU. You're strange.

JACK. From walking behind you.

LULU. Why are you staring?

JACK. I've got one shilling, that's all.

LULU. You're excited.

JACK. It's three years since I slept with a girl.

LULU. Come on . . . give me the shilling.

JACK. What did you live on, before?

LULU. I was a parlourmaid.

JACK. Parlour-maids have rougher hands than you.

LULU. I had a rich friend. Give me your shilling.

JACK. You loved too much already.

LULU. Yes.

> JACK *takes out his wallet*.

JACK. I want sixpence change.

LULU. I haven't got it.

JACK. I must take a bus in the morning.

LULU. Why are you trembling?

JACK. Look in your pocket.

> *She does*.

LULU. There's nothing.

JACK. Let me look.

LULU. This is all I've got.

> *She takes a ten-shilling piece out of her pocket*.

Ten shillings.

JACK. Give it to me.

LULU. I'll change it in the morning.

JACK. No, give it me now.

LULU. You're richer than me.

JACK. But I'm staying all night.

> *She gives him the money and picks up the lamp*. JACK *sees the portrait*.

JACK. You were a society lady. You took care of yourself in those days.

LULU *opens the bedroom door.*

LULU. Come in.

JACK. We don't need the light.

LULU. In the dark?

JACK. Why not? The lamp's going out. It stinks.

LULU. Let it burn.

JACK. The moon is shining.

LULU. Come on.

JACK. As you like.

LULU. Why don't you come?

JACK. I'm afraid.

LULU *falls on him and kisses him.*

LULU. I wouldn't do you any harm. I love you. You're like a baby. You look puzzled. Why don't you look at me?

JACK. I ask myself, whether or not I will succeed.

LULU. You too?

She puts her hand under his overcoat.

What do you want of me? Don't make me beg you. Don't be afraid.

JACK. Aren't you ashamed, to sell your love?

LULU. What else can I do?

JACK. You could do better than this. I never found a more beautiful girl in the street.

LULU *holds him in her embrace.*

LULU. Come on. I'm not as bad as I look.

JACK. All right.

He follows her into the bedroom. GESCHWITZ, *left alone, writes a message with her index finger on the floorboards:*

GESCHWITZ. You planted it in my heart . . . this love . . . my holy child . . .

The lamp goes out. The room is dark except that, now, the floor is illuminated by two squares of light from the windows.

. . . when it grows dark . . . she is my only thought . . . especially when it's dark . . . if she'd never married . . . then I'd never have met her . . . or if my father had never married . . . then I'd never have seen her . . . why am I crippled? . . . I'll never marry . . .

There is a crash from the bedroom.

Lulu?

LULU, *half-dressed and bleeding, bursts out of the bedroom. She tries to hold the door closed behind her. Inside,* JACK *is trying to get out.*

LULU. Help! Help!

GESCHWITZ *grabs her revolver. Aims it at the door.*

GESCHWITZ. Let him out!

JACK *comes pelting out of the bedroom, bent double. He stabs* GESCHWITZ. *She collapses, firing a shot at the ceiling.*

LULU. Oh God!

JACK *seizes* GESCHWITZ *by the leather strap and takes the revolver off her.*

Police! Police!

JACK. Be quiet!

He runs to the exit door, barring LULU *from escaping.*

GESCHWITZ. He won't shoot!

JACK *rushes at* LULU, *grabs her.*

JACK. Got you!

LULU. He's trying to cut my stomach open!

JACK. Quiet!

He throws himself on the floor and tries to embrace her feet.

LULU. Murder! Murder!

She gets away. JACK *rushes to the exit door. He's breathing heavily, his hands dripping with blood.* LULU *looks round, sees the whisky-bottle. She smashes it against the table and charges at* JACK *with the remnant.* JACK *meets her with his foot and sends her crashing to the floor.*

LULU. Oh . . . oh . . . help me . . .

JACK *composes himself, lifts her up and carries her into the bedroom. After a moment,* LULU *is heard screaming.*

He's cutting me! He's cutting me!

GESCHWITZ. Lulu . . . I can't . . .

LULU *screams terribly.*

LULU. No, don't! Don't!

A few seconds pass. JACK *re-emerges, carrying a small packet wrapped in newspaper. He goes into the bedroom.* LULU *can still be heard groaning.*

GESCHWITZ. Lulu . . . my love.

JACK *returns carrying the washbasin. He washes the blood from his hands. Looks at the newspaper-wrapped packet.*

JACK. Amazing. I've never seen one like it. After I'm dead, when my collection's put up for auction, the Medical Association will pay three hundred pounds for this. They'll say 'That's one in a million!'

He looks round for something to dry his hands on.

How poor they are. Not even a towel.

He pulls up GESCHWITZ's *dress and wipes his hands on her white petticoat. To* GESCHWITZ.

It won't be long now.

He goes. GESCHWITZ *crawls towards the bedroom door, leaving a trail of blood behind her.*

GESCHWITZ. Once more . . . my angel . . . let me see you again . . . once more . . . I love . . . I love . . .

Her elbows give way.

Ssh . . .

She dies.

End of play.